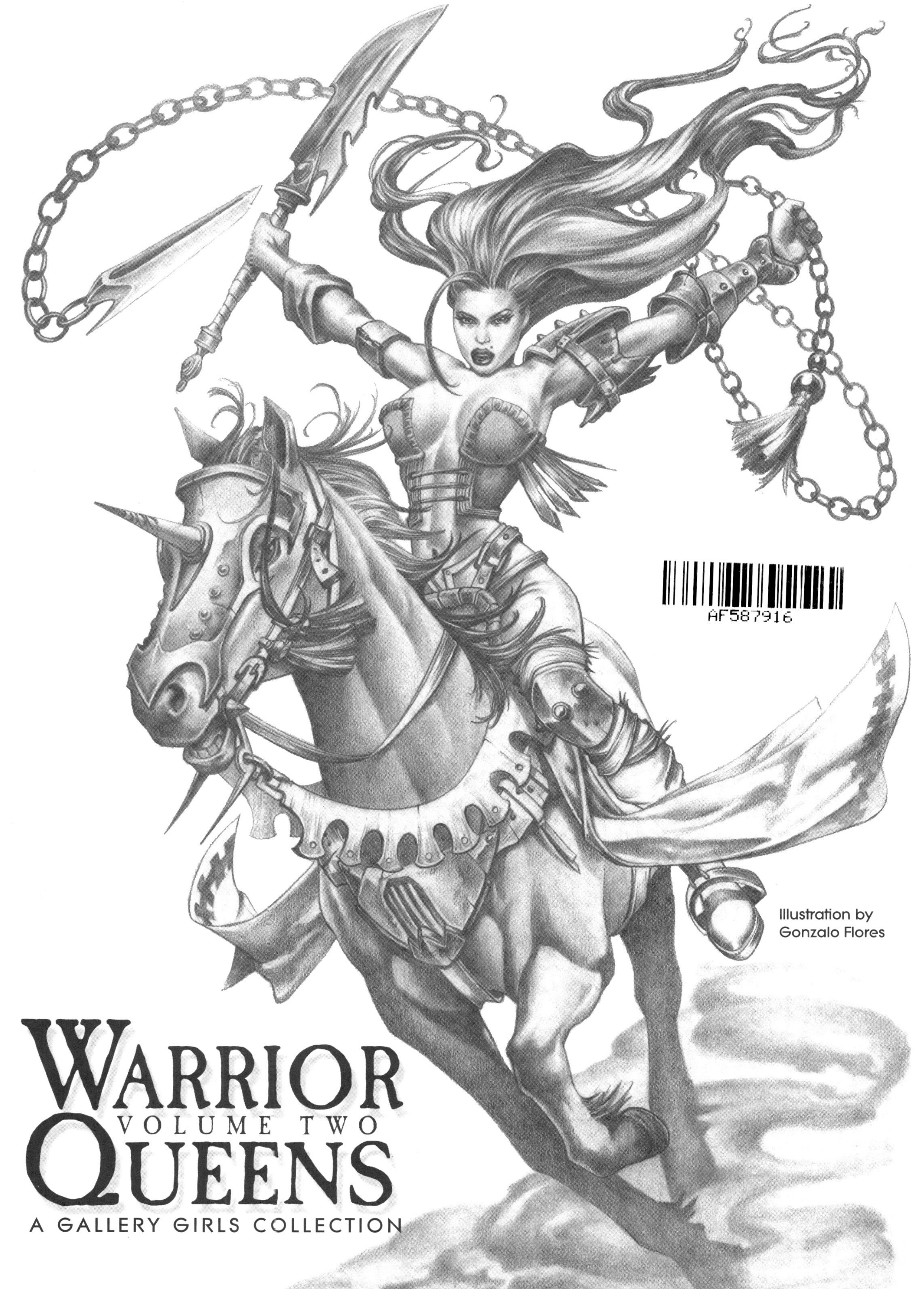
AF587916
Illustration by
Gonzalo Flores
WARRIOR
VOLUME TWO
QUEENS
A GALLERY GIRLS COLLECTION

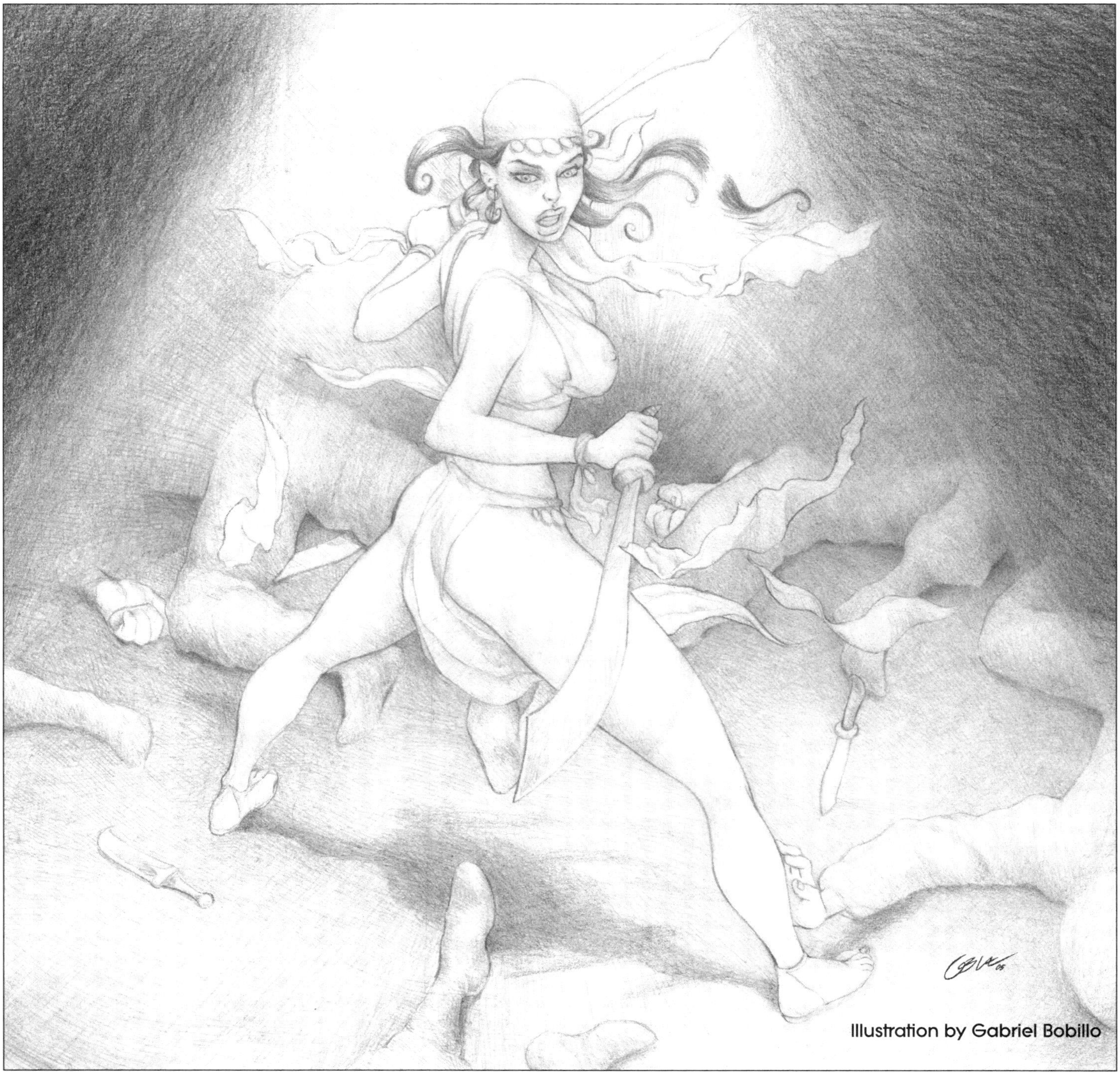

Illustration by Gabriel Bobillo

WARRIOR QUEENS

Volume Two

Book design by Grassy Knoll Studios.

Published by
SQP Inc.
PO Box 248 - Columbus, NJ 08022

Sal Quartuccio & Bob Keenan - Publishers

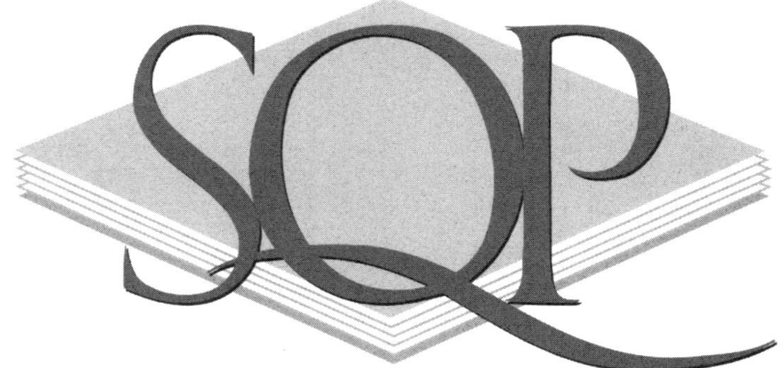

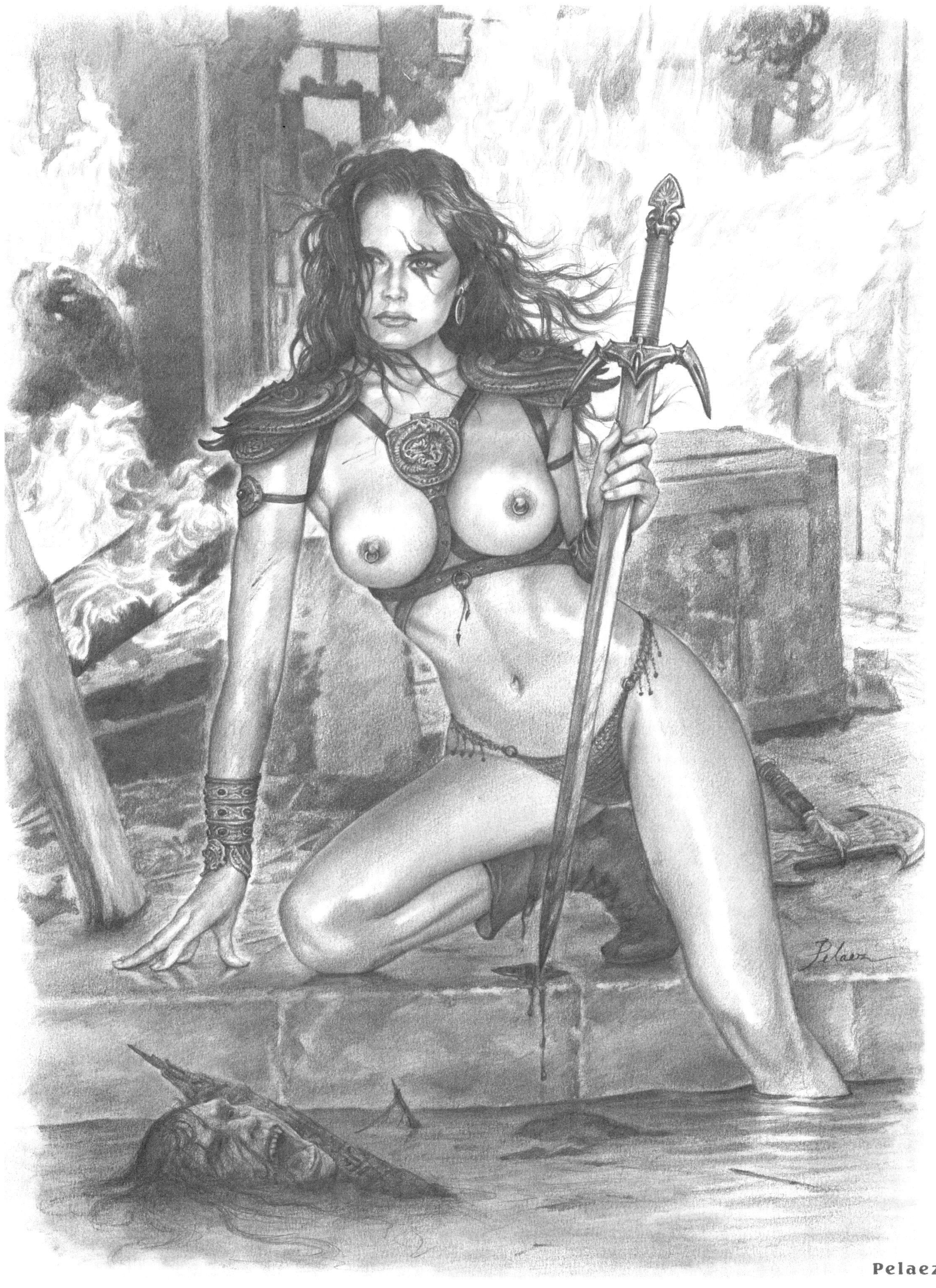

Pelaez

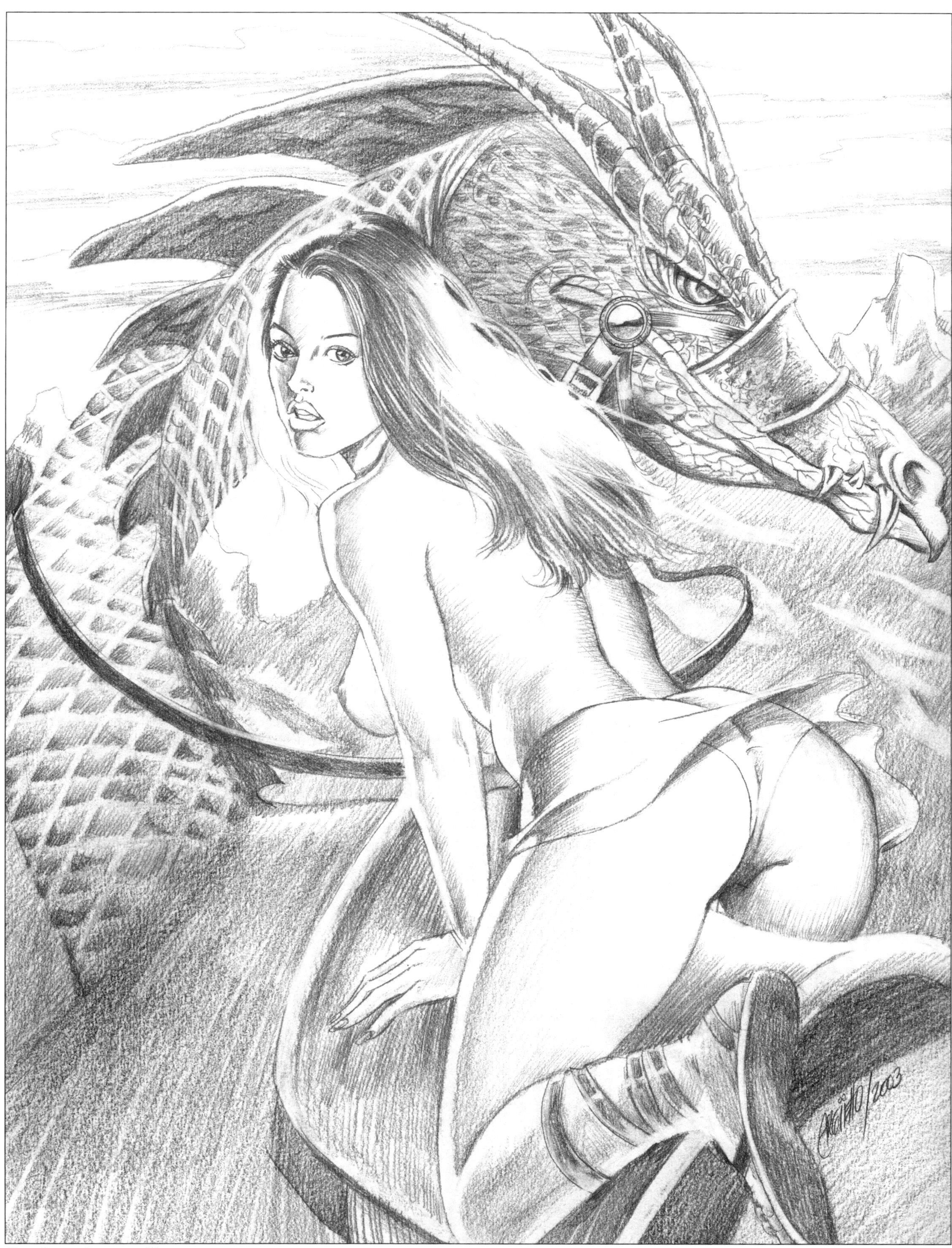

Carlos Arguello

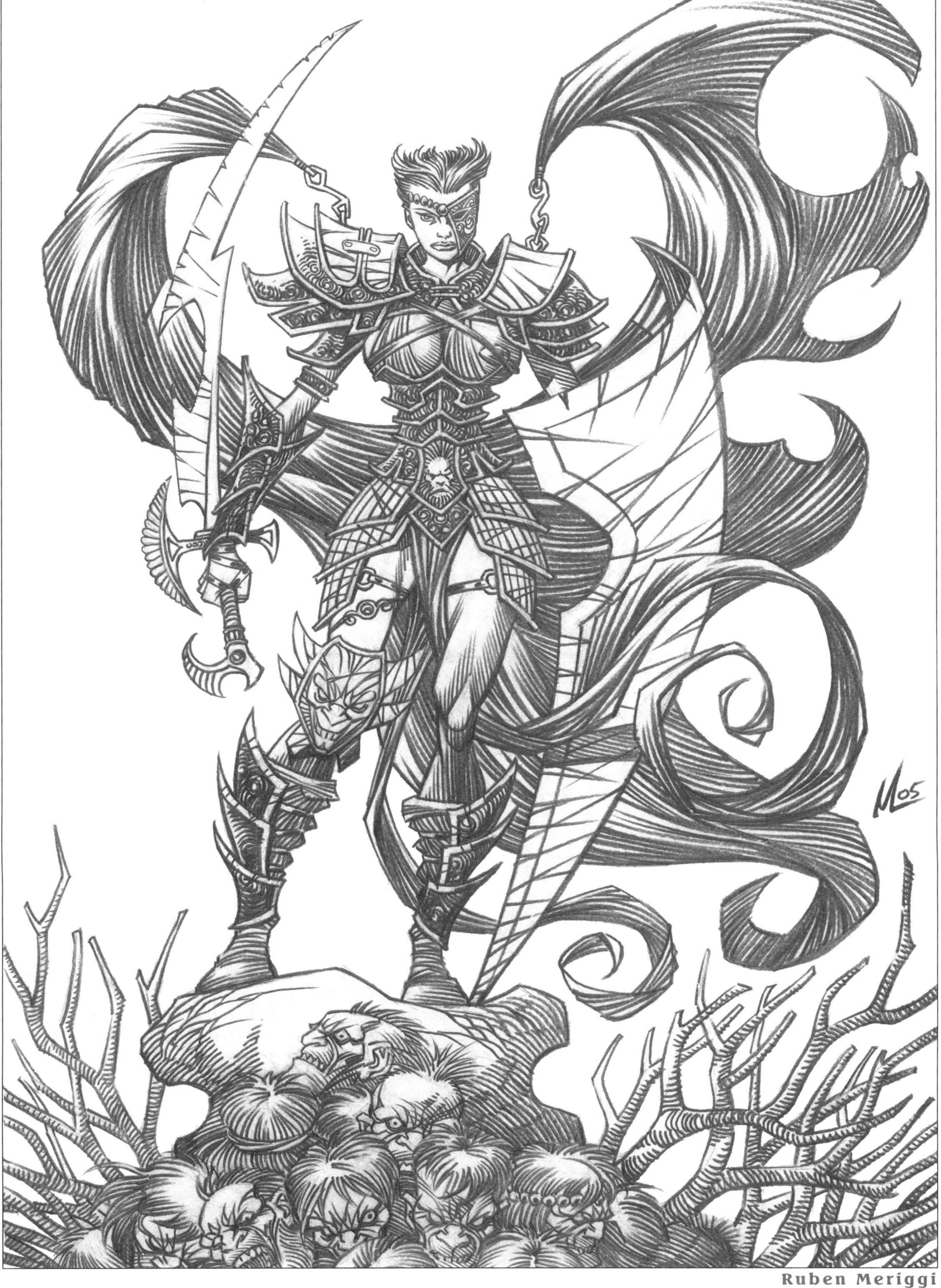

Ruben Meriggi

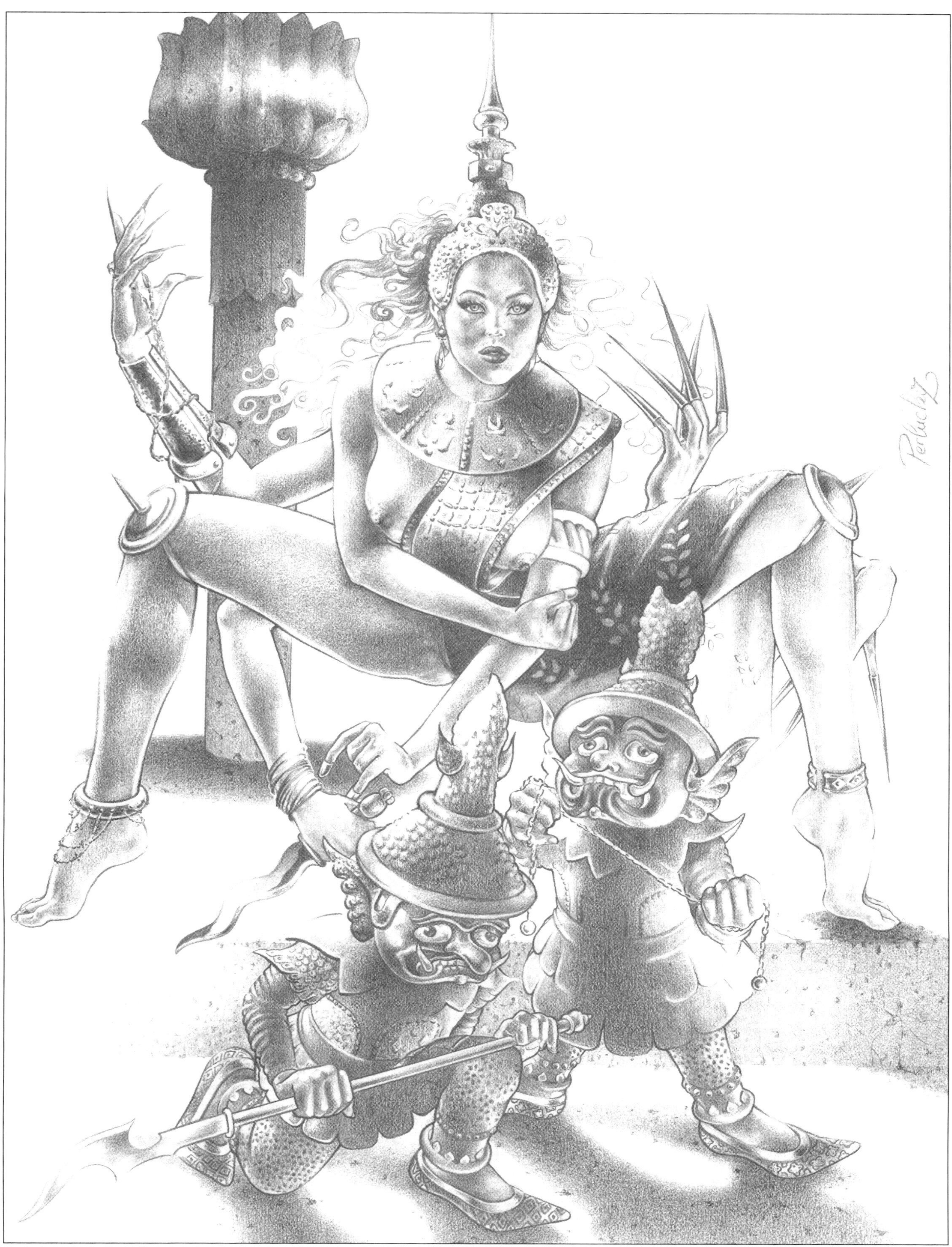

Perla Perlucky

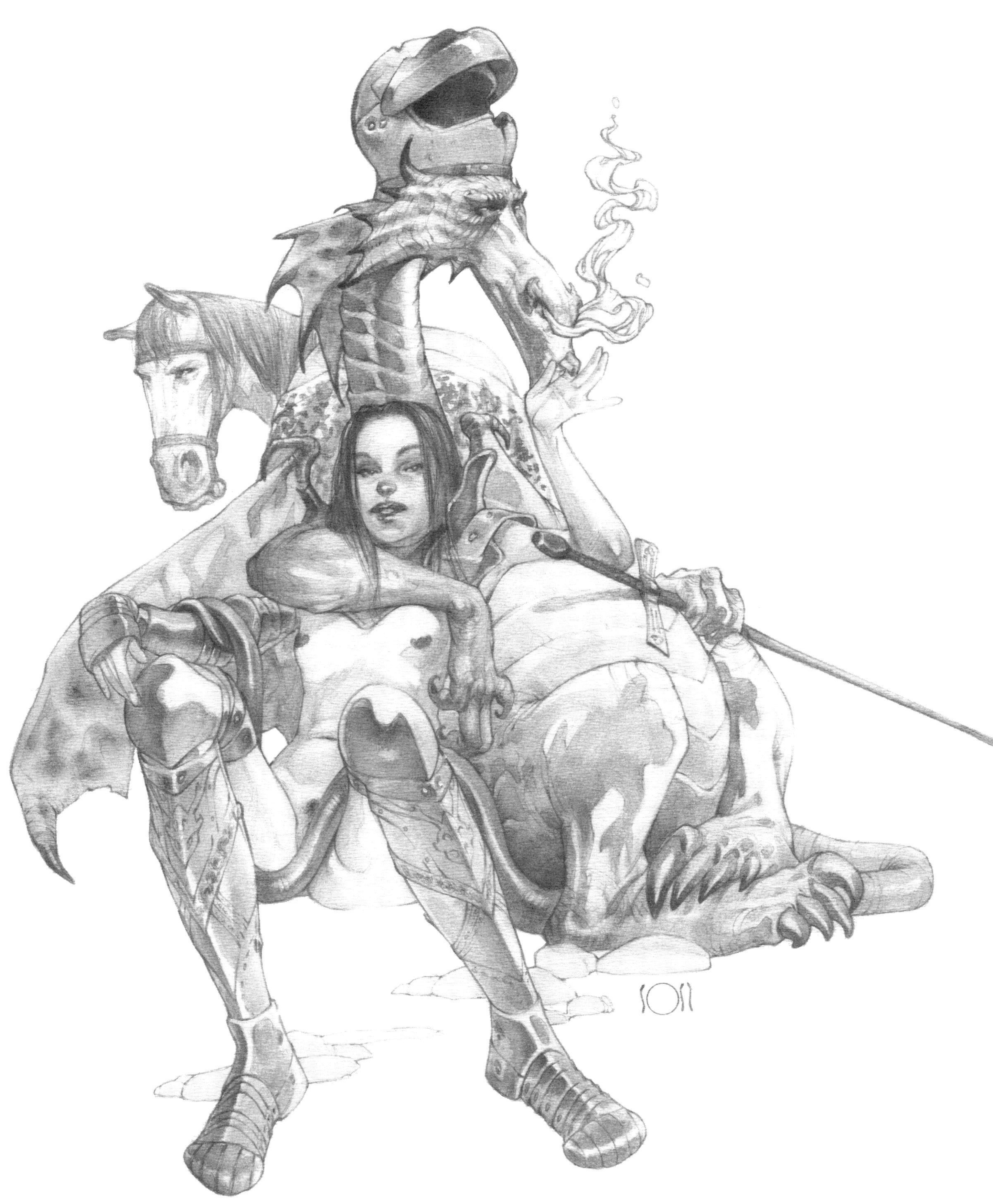

Marcelo Sosa

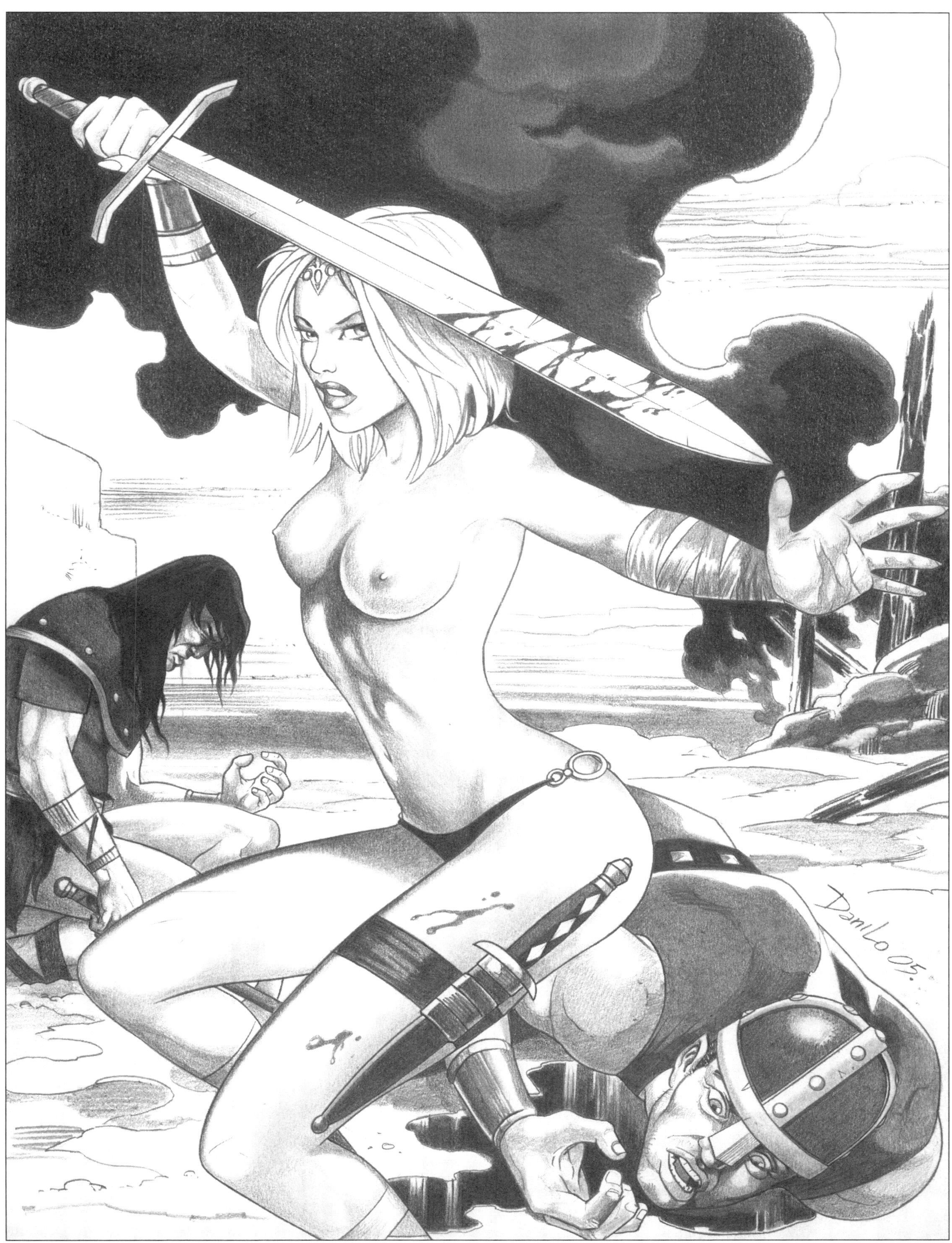

Danilo Guida

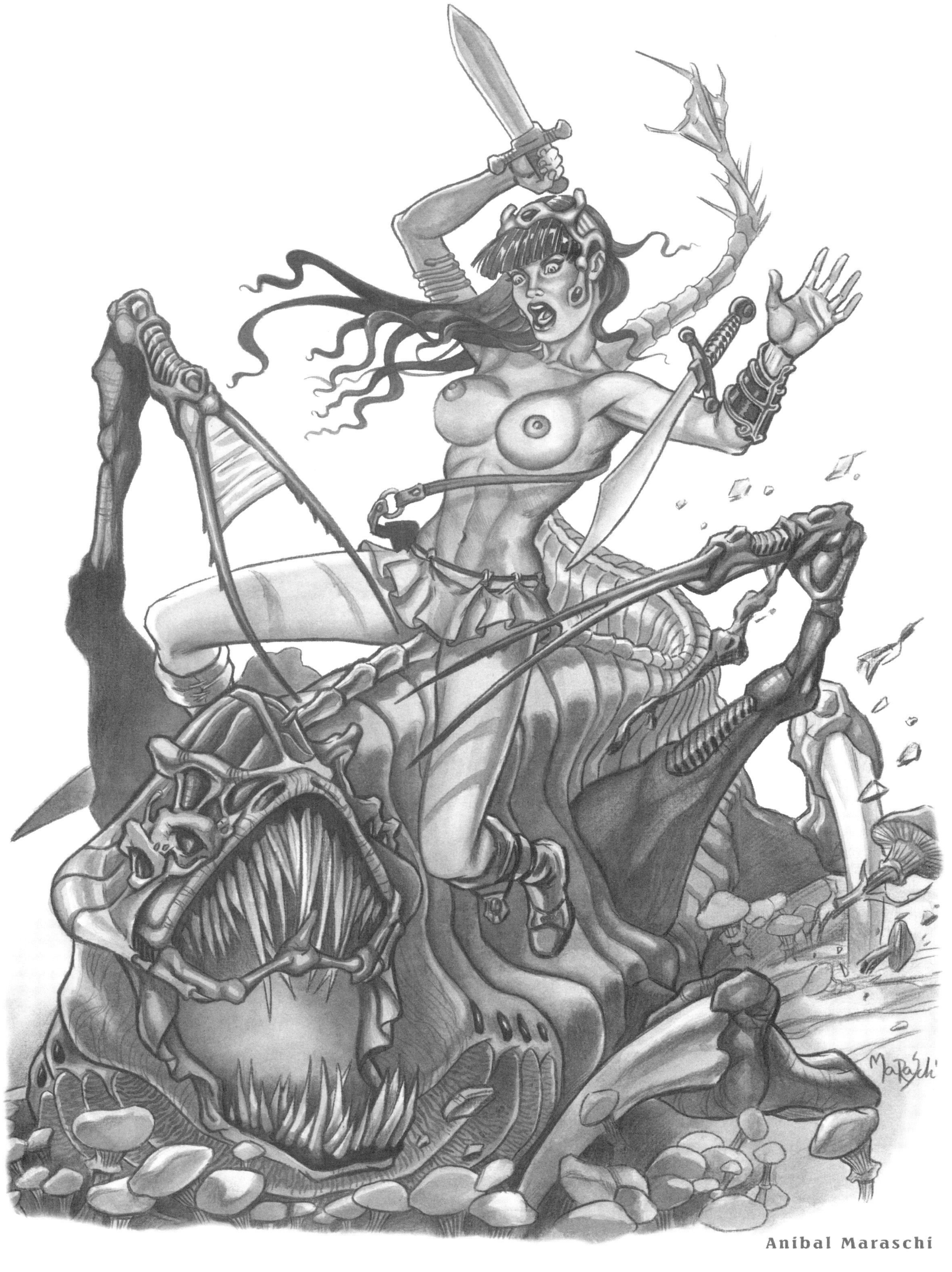

Anibal Maraschi

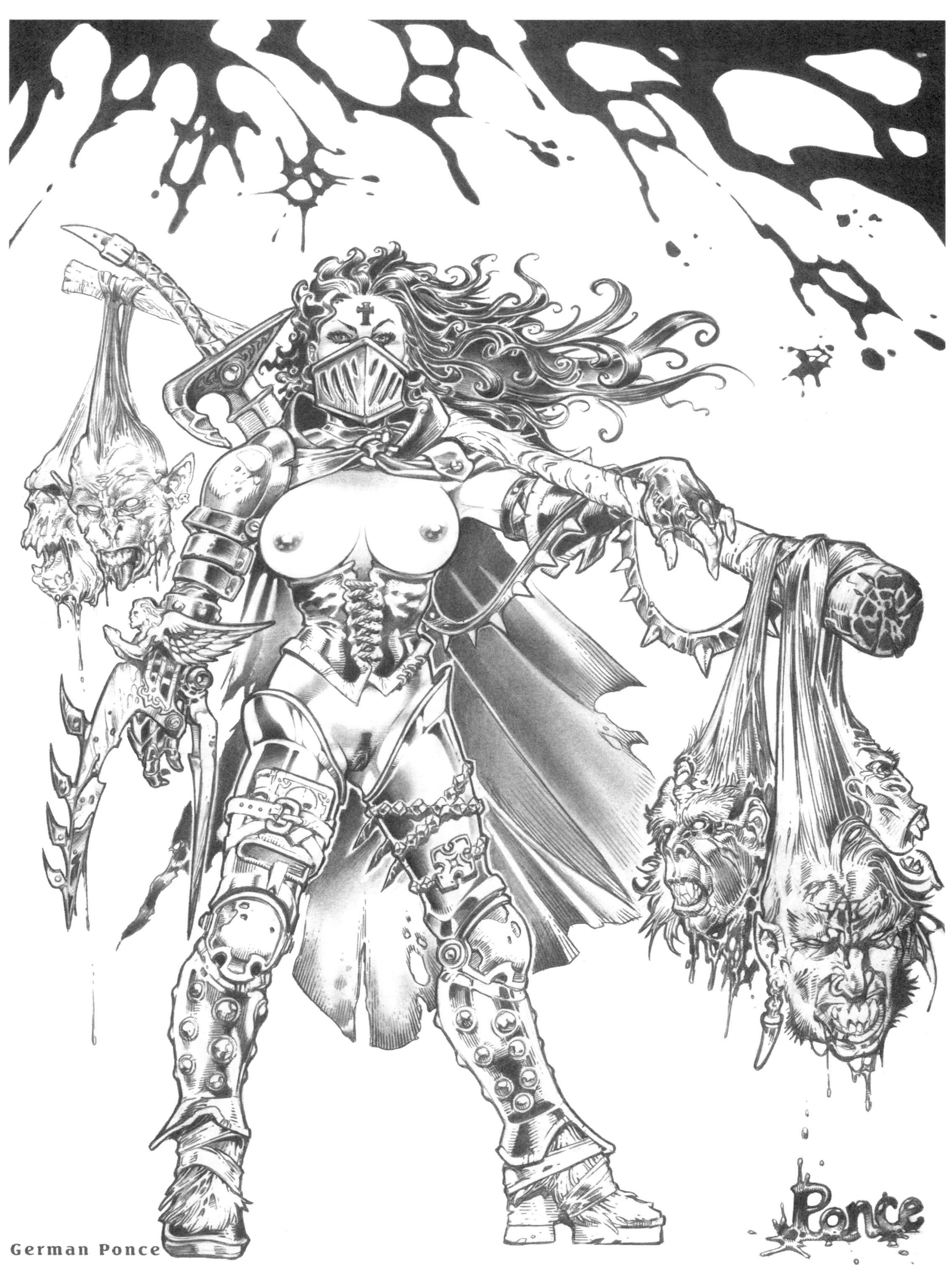

German Ponce

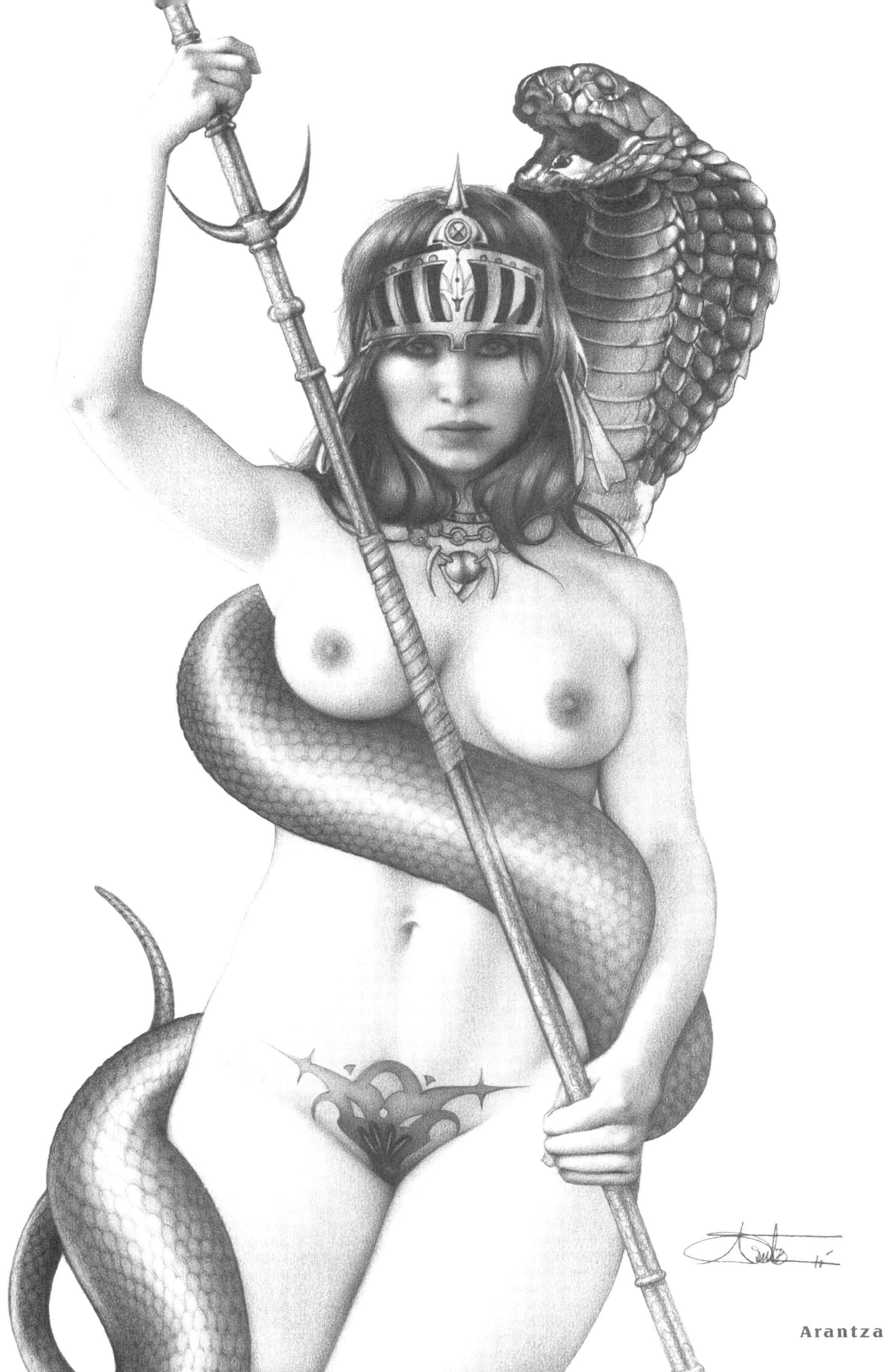

Arantza

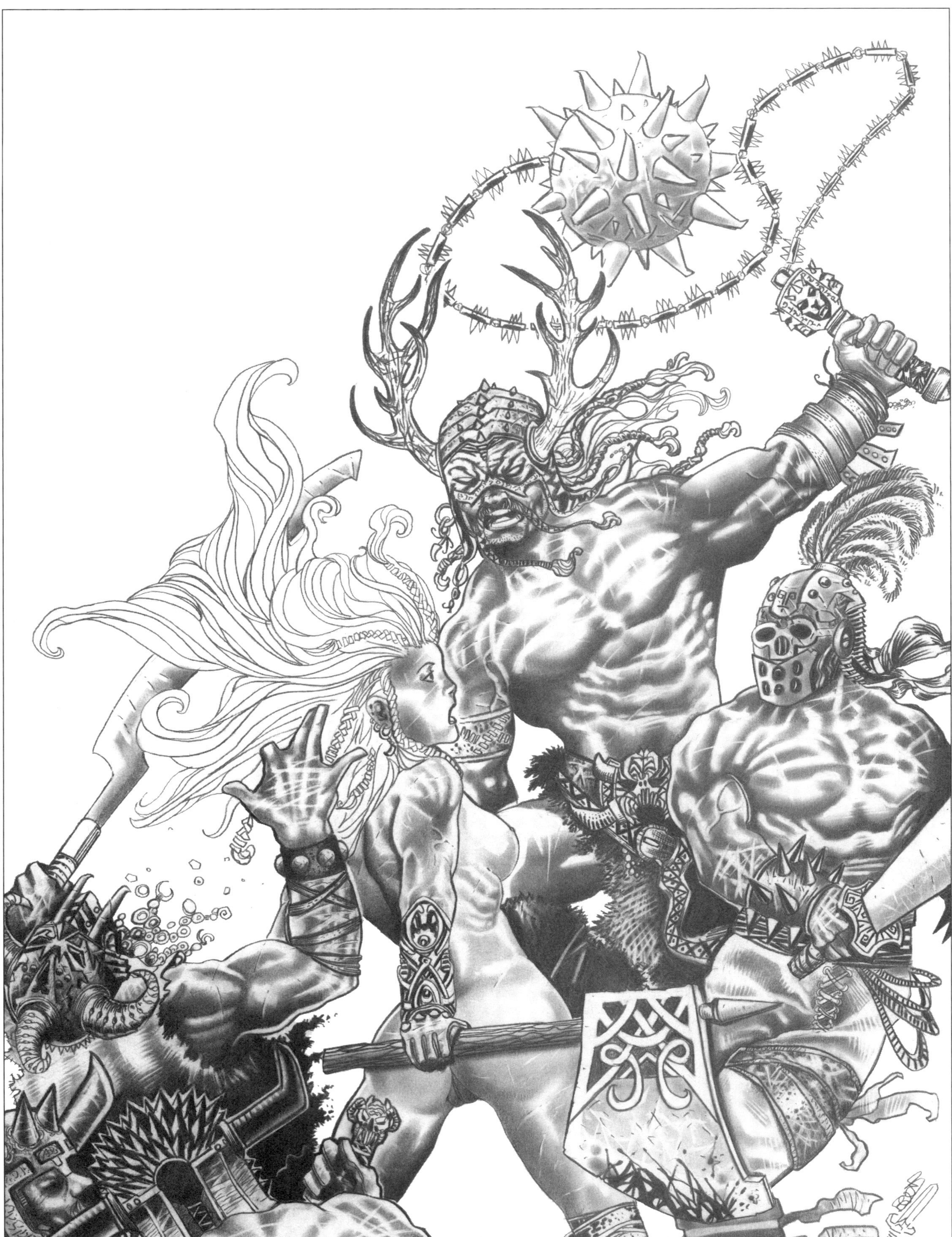

Luis Buci

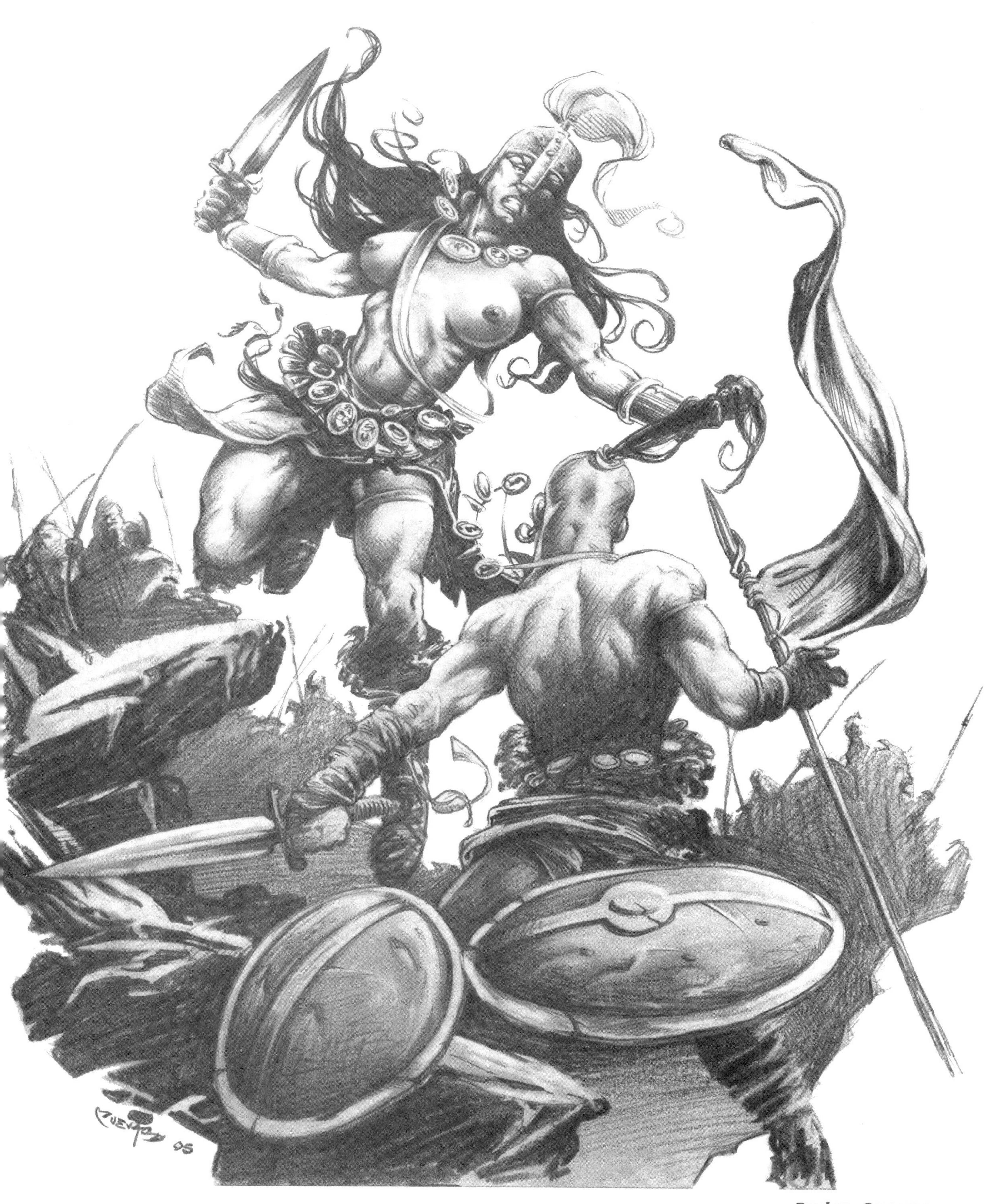

Pedro Cuevas

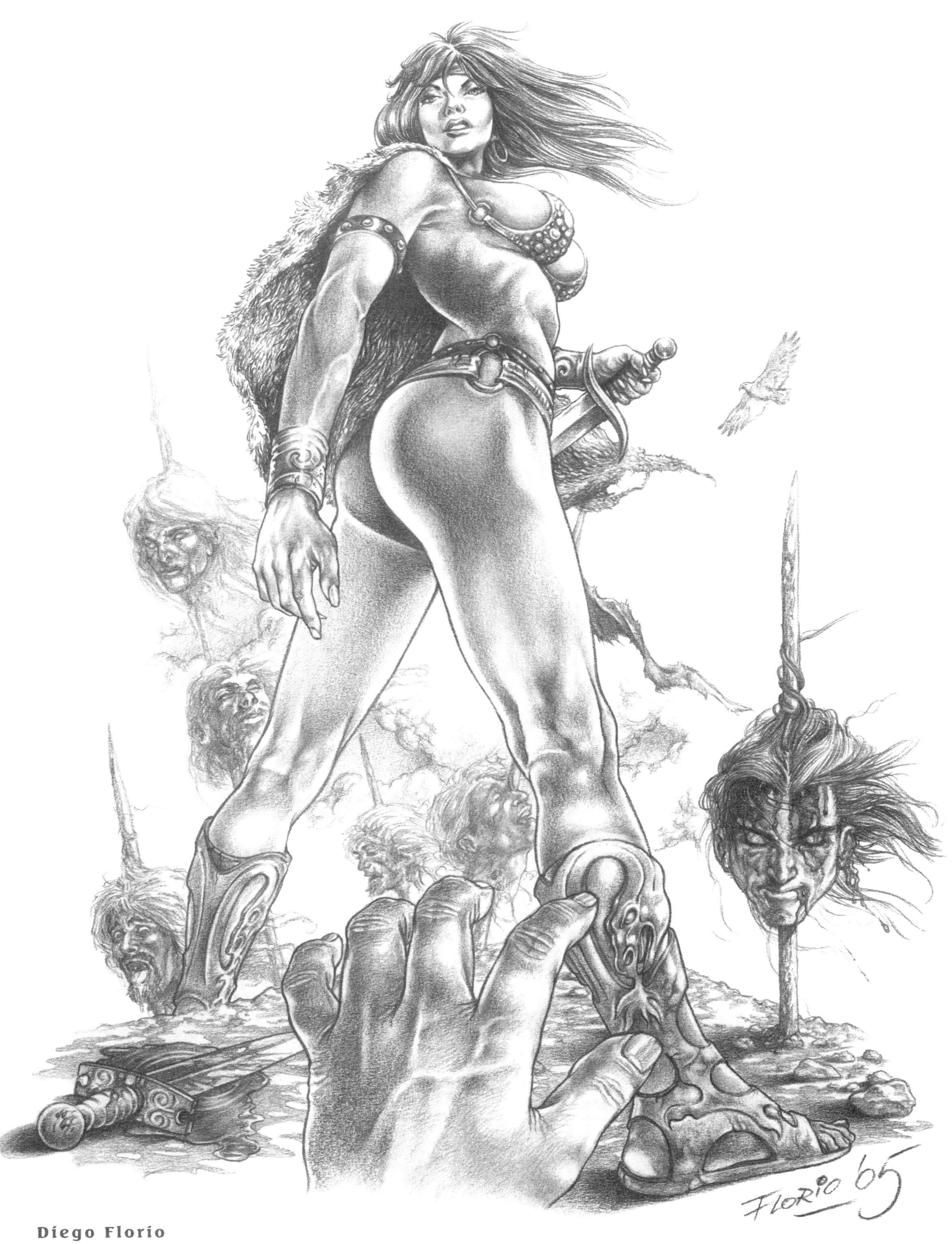

Diego Florio

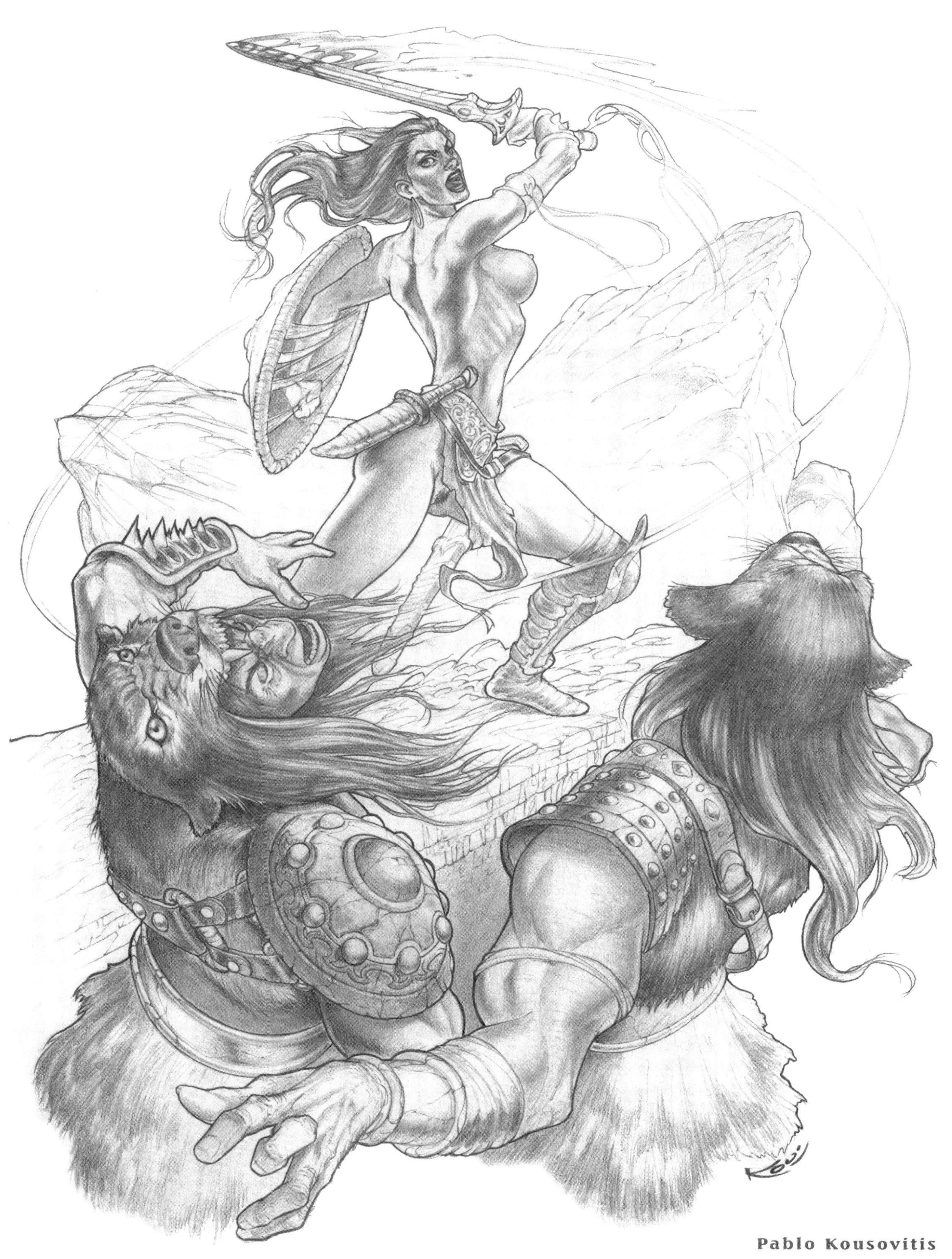

Pablo Kousovitis

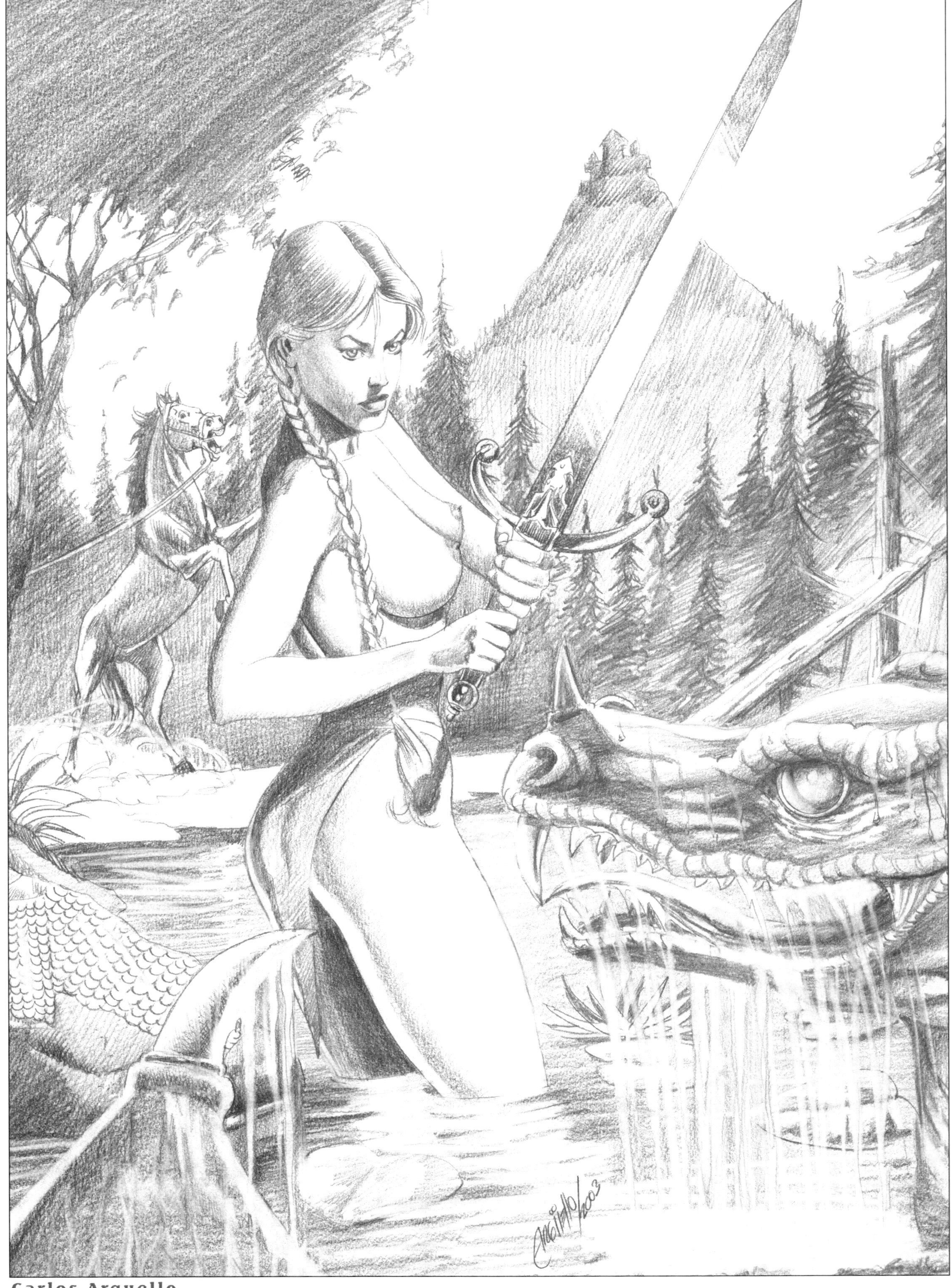

Carlos Arguello

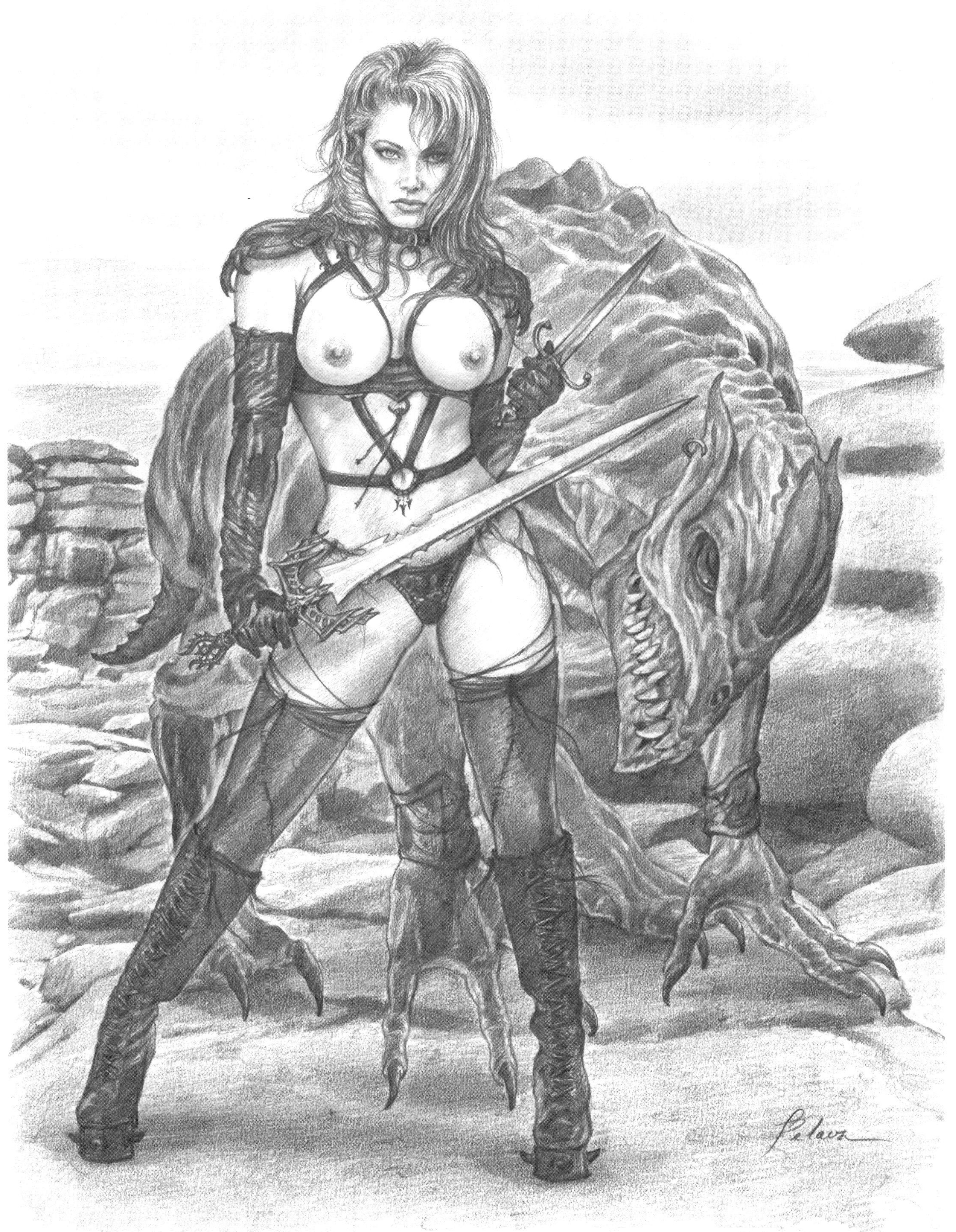

Pelaez

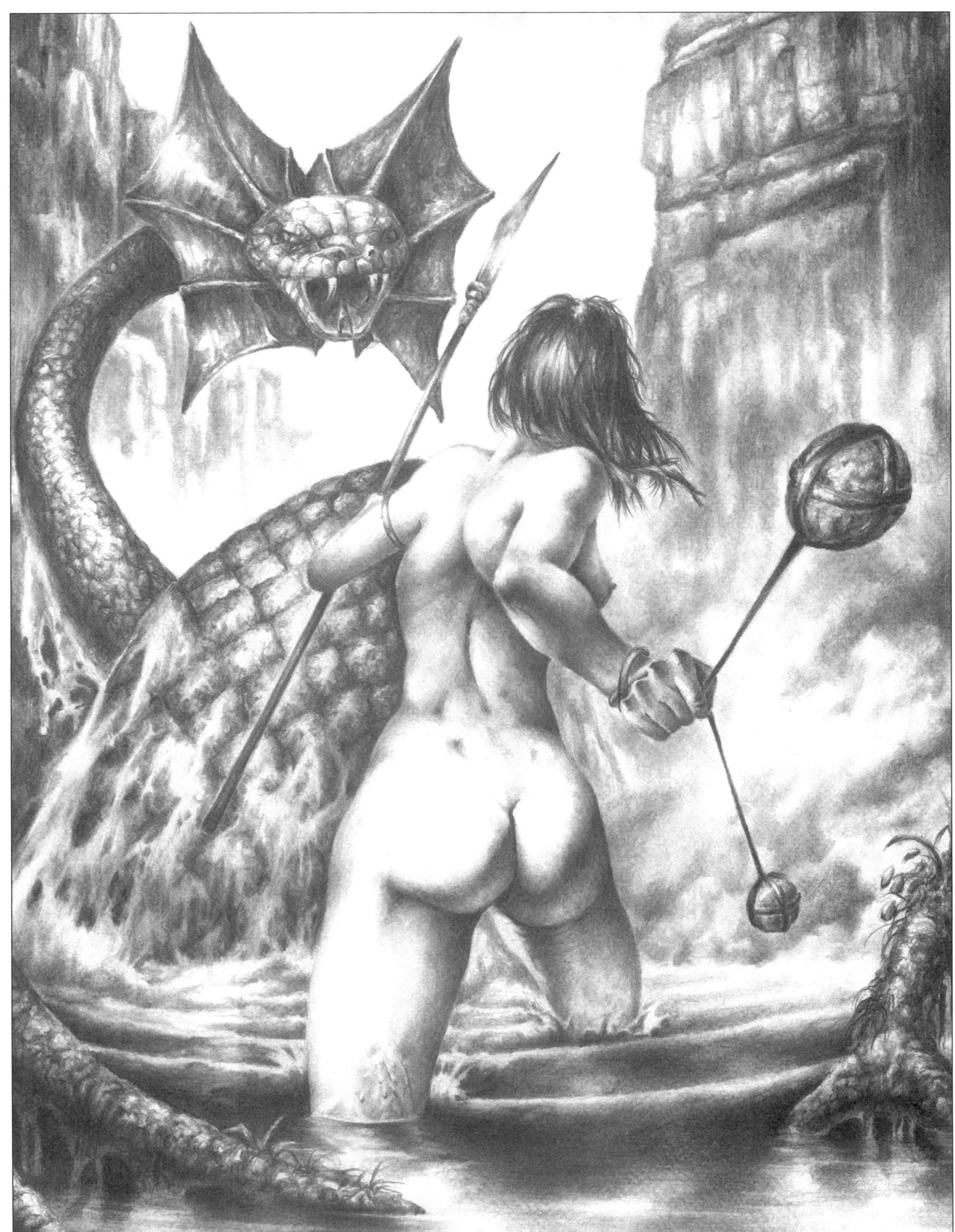

Diego Candia

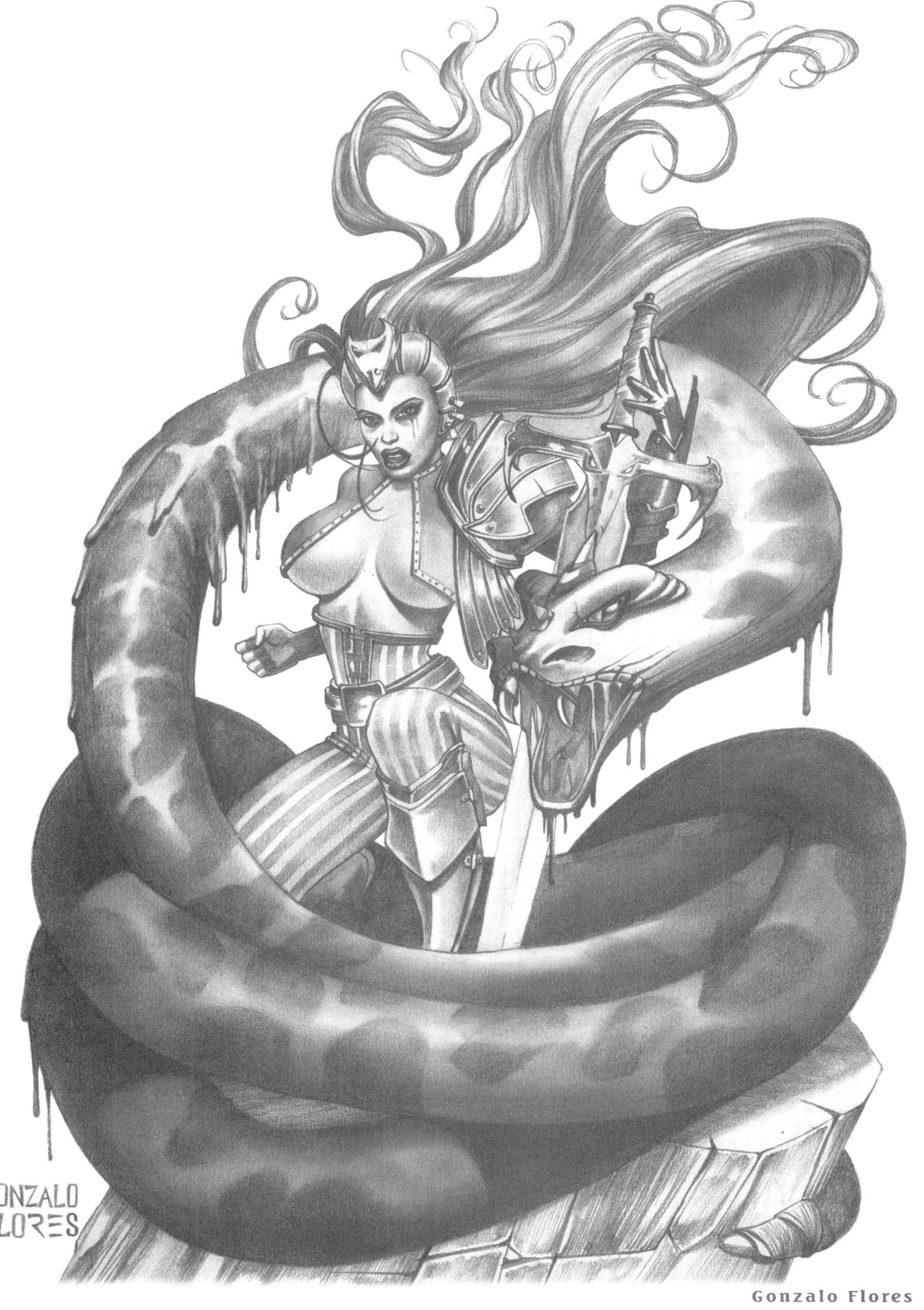

Gonzalo Flores

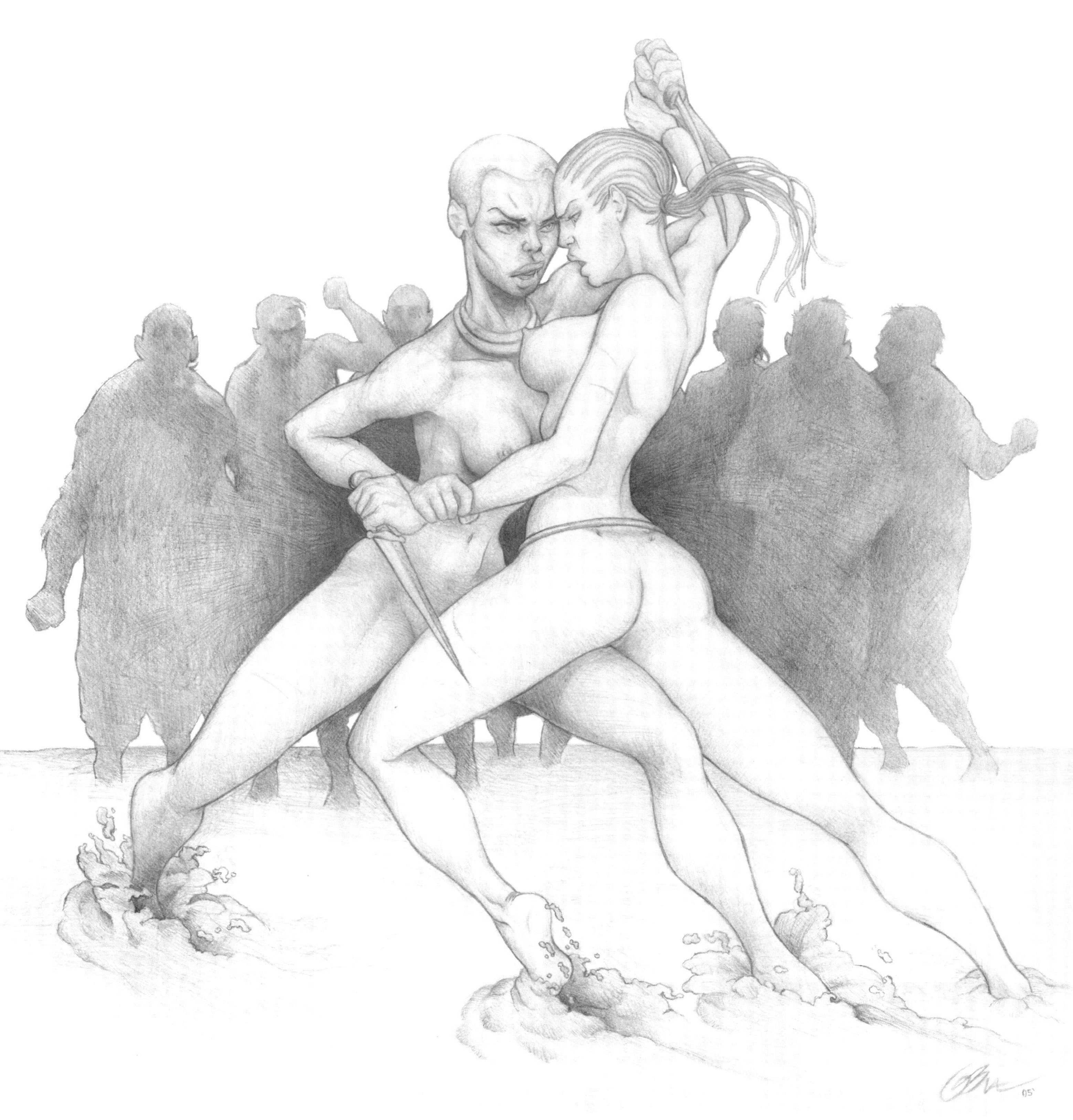

Gabriel Bobillo

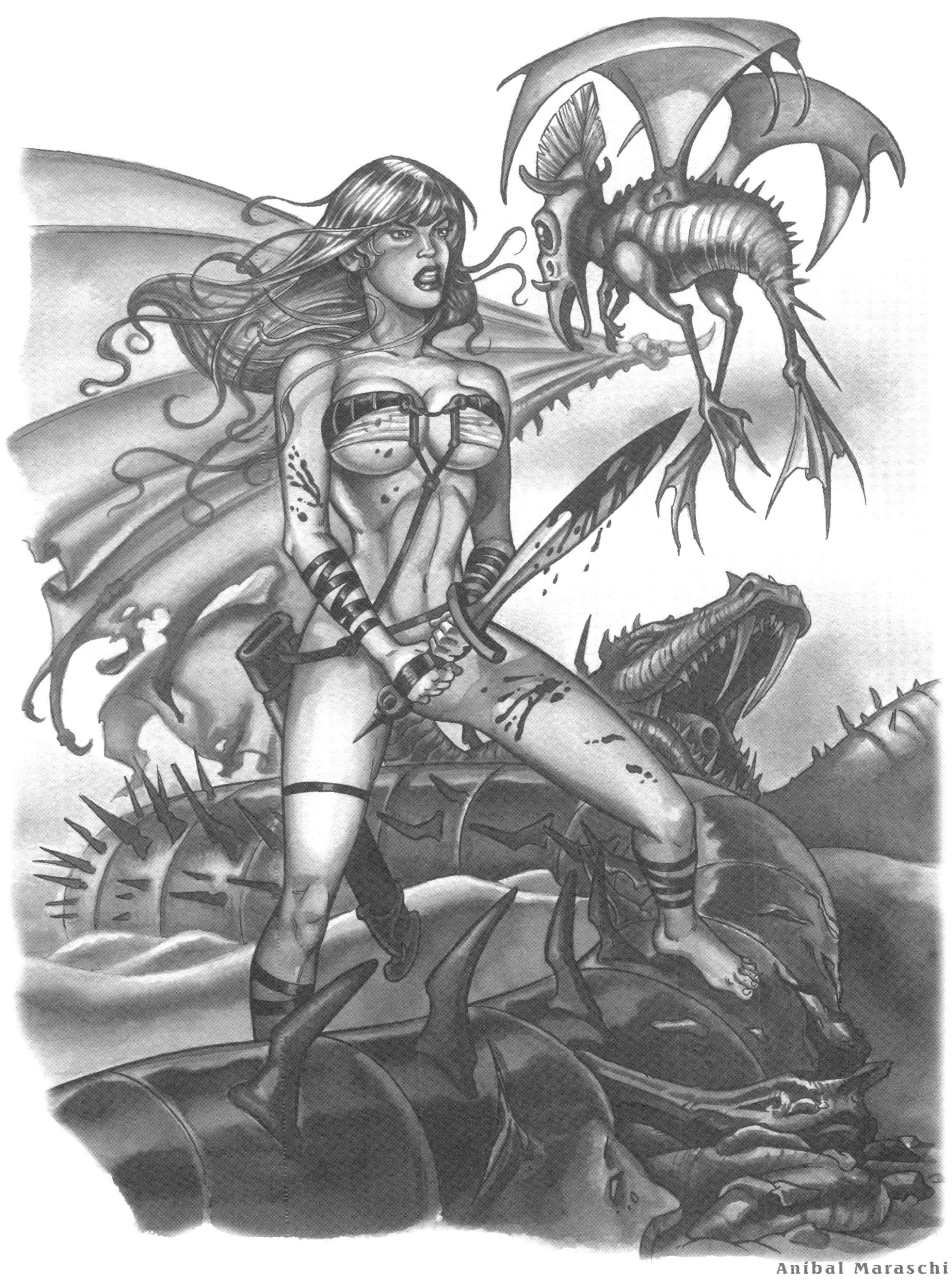

Anibal Maraschi

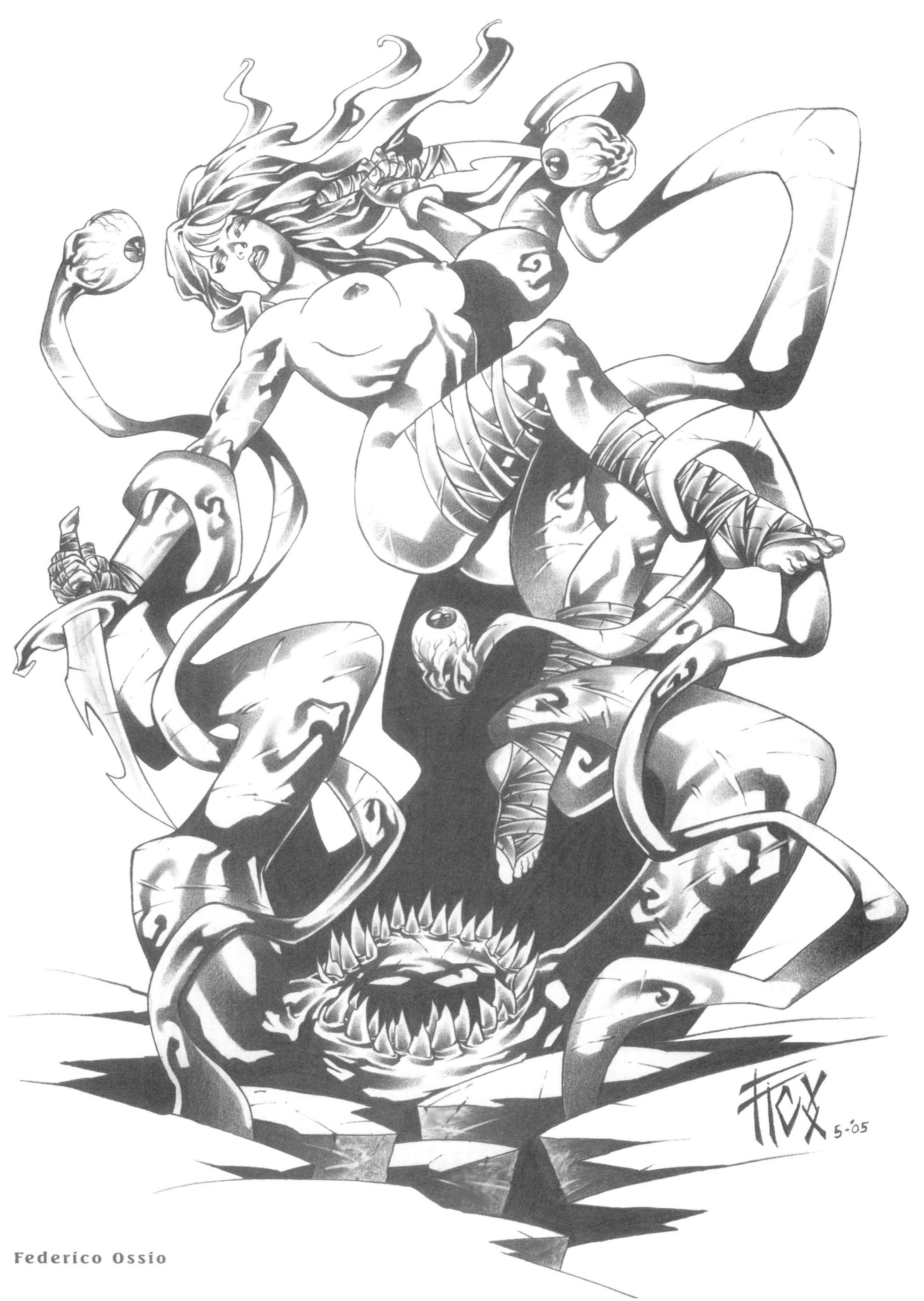

Federico Ossio

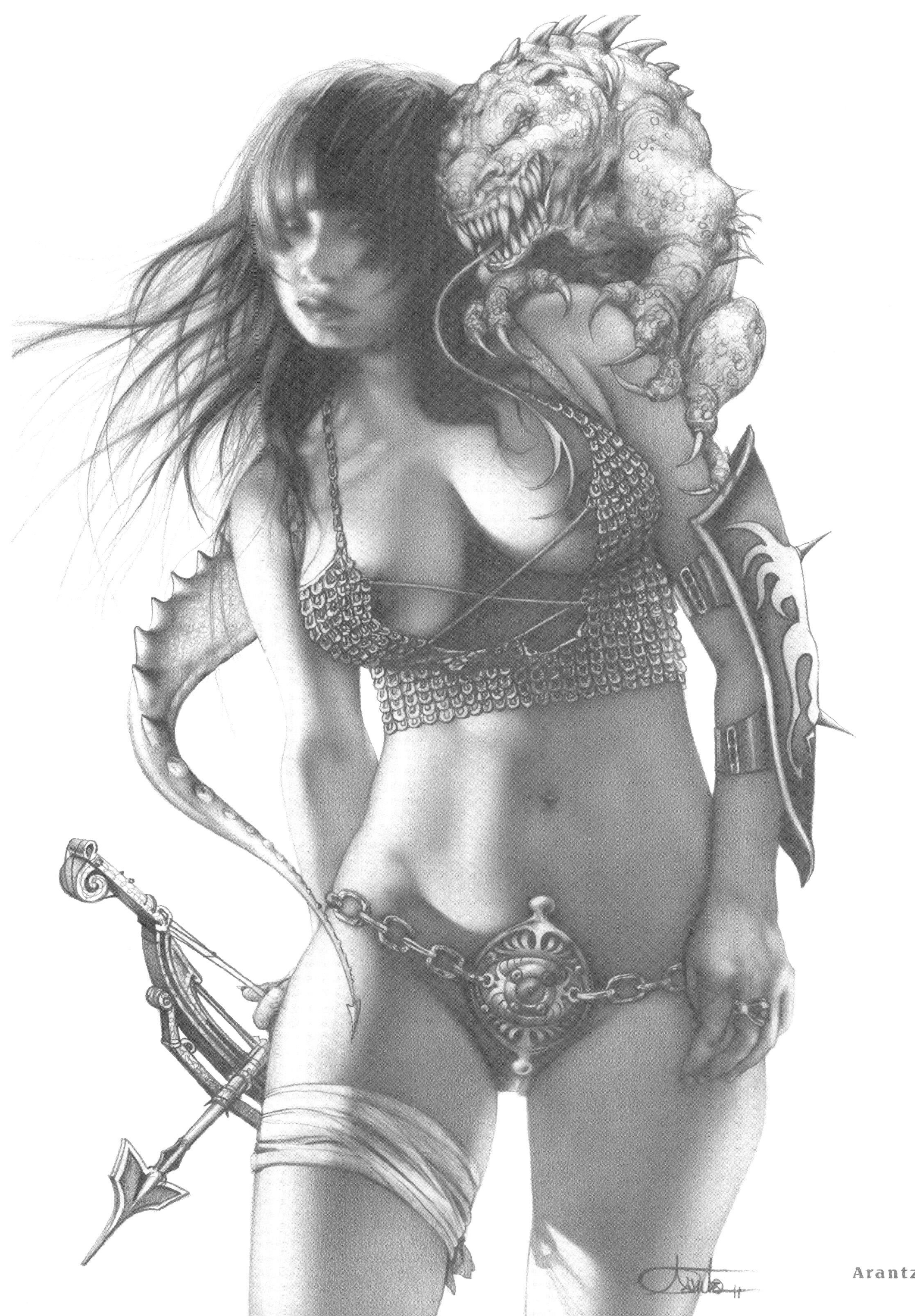

Arantza

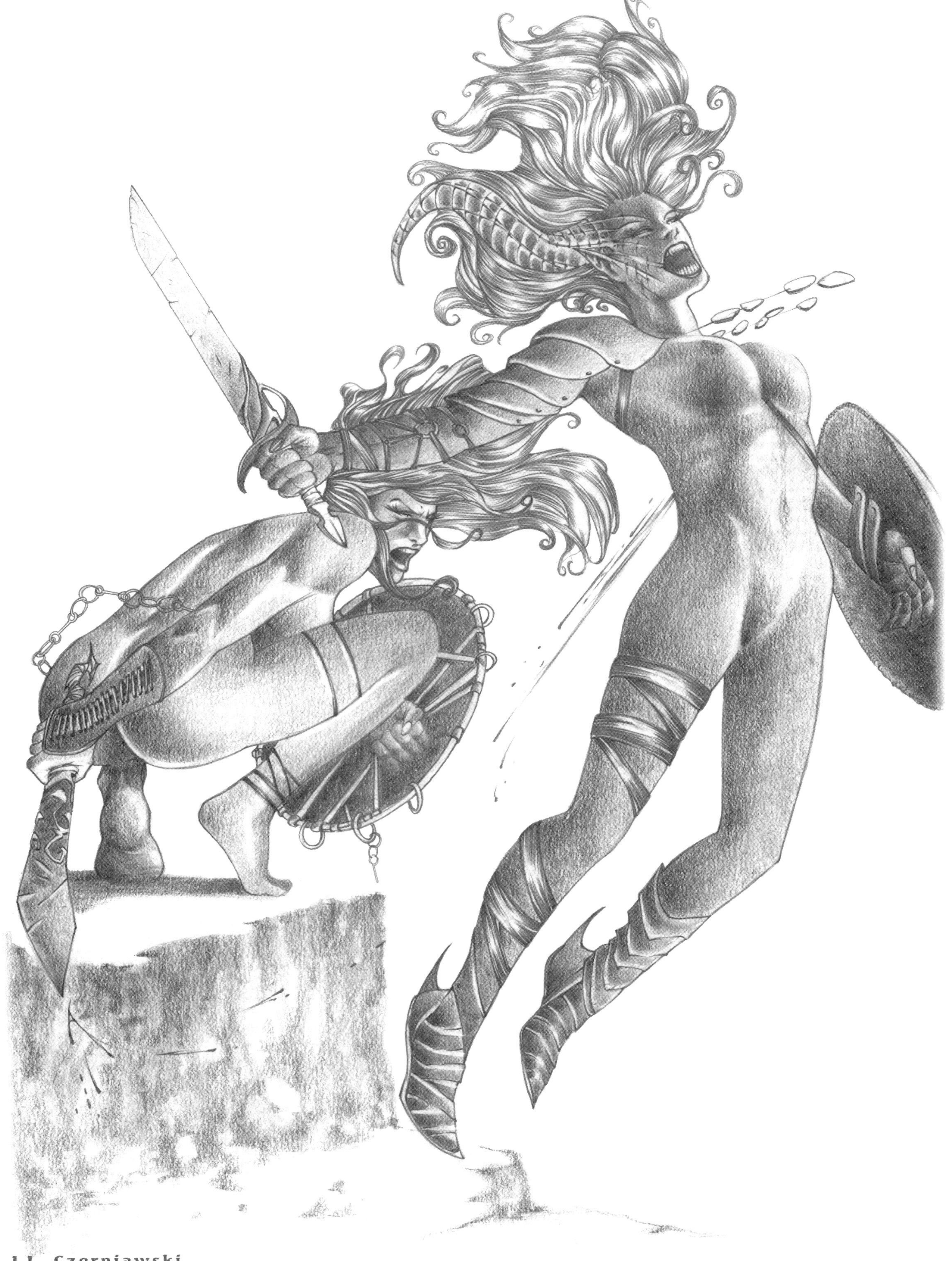

J.L. Czerniawski

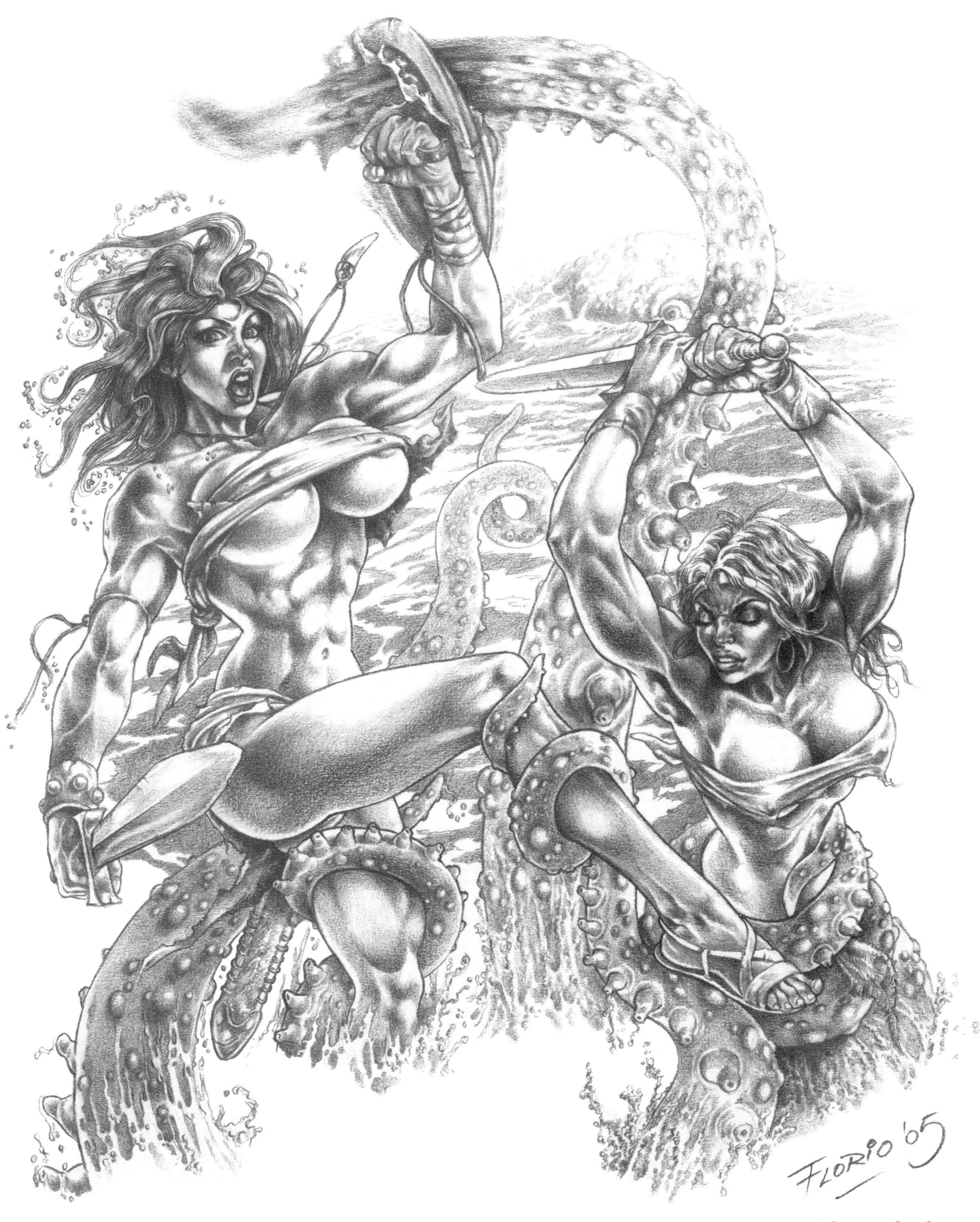

Diego Florio

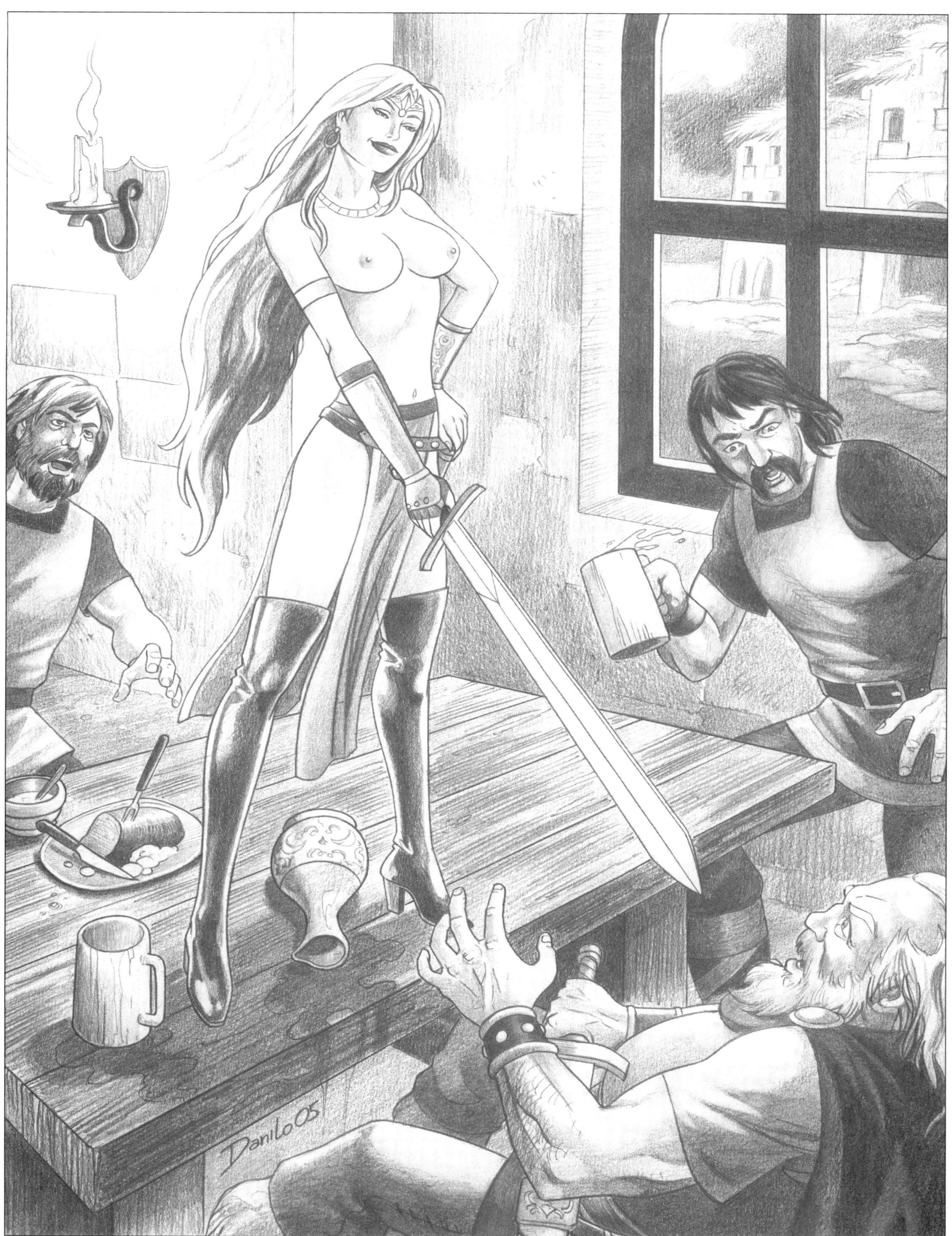

Danilo Guída

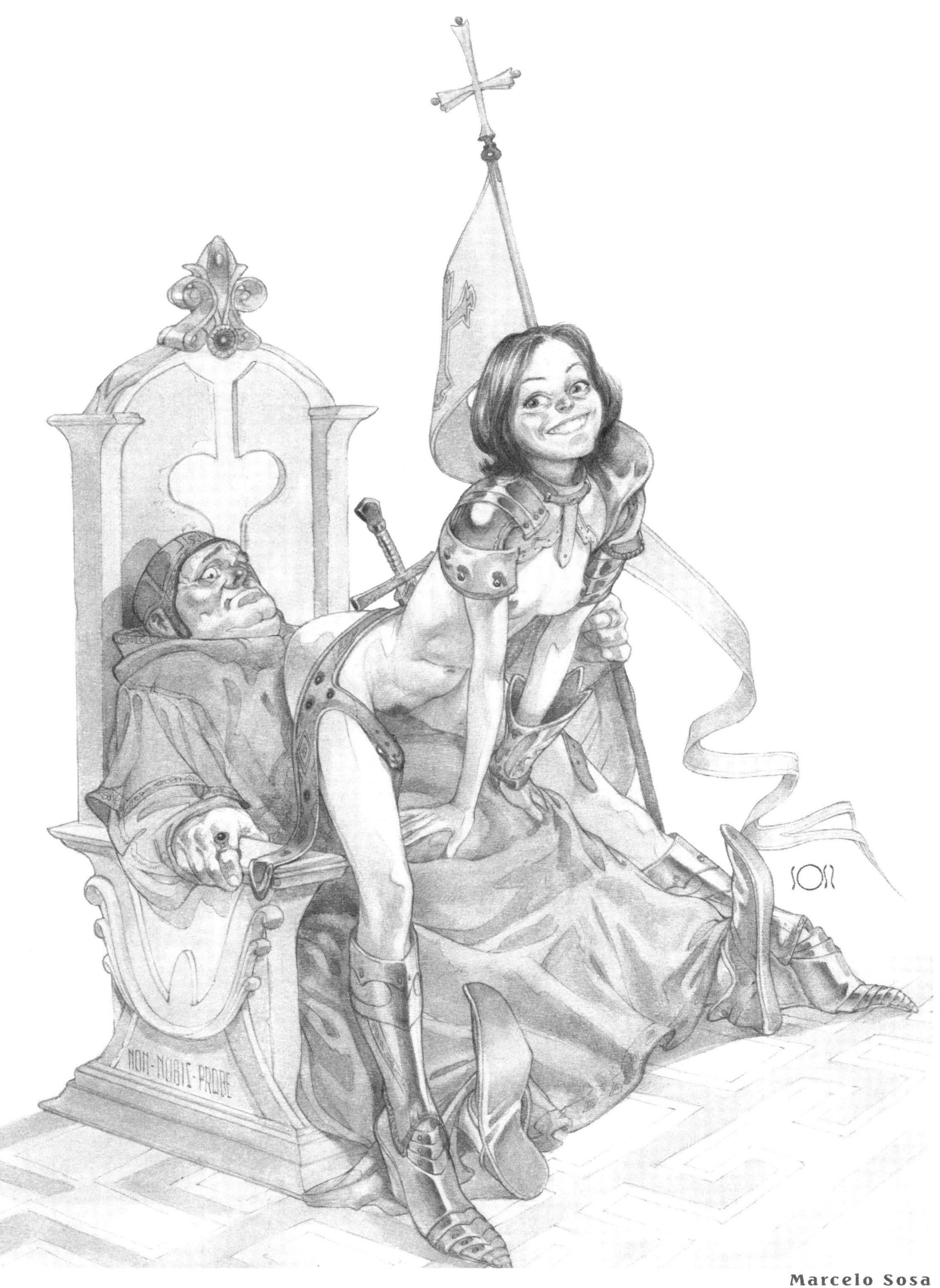

Marcelo Sosa

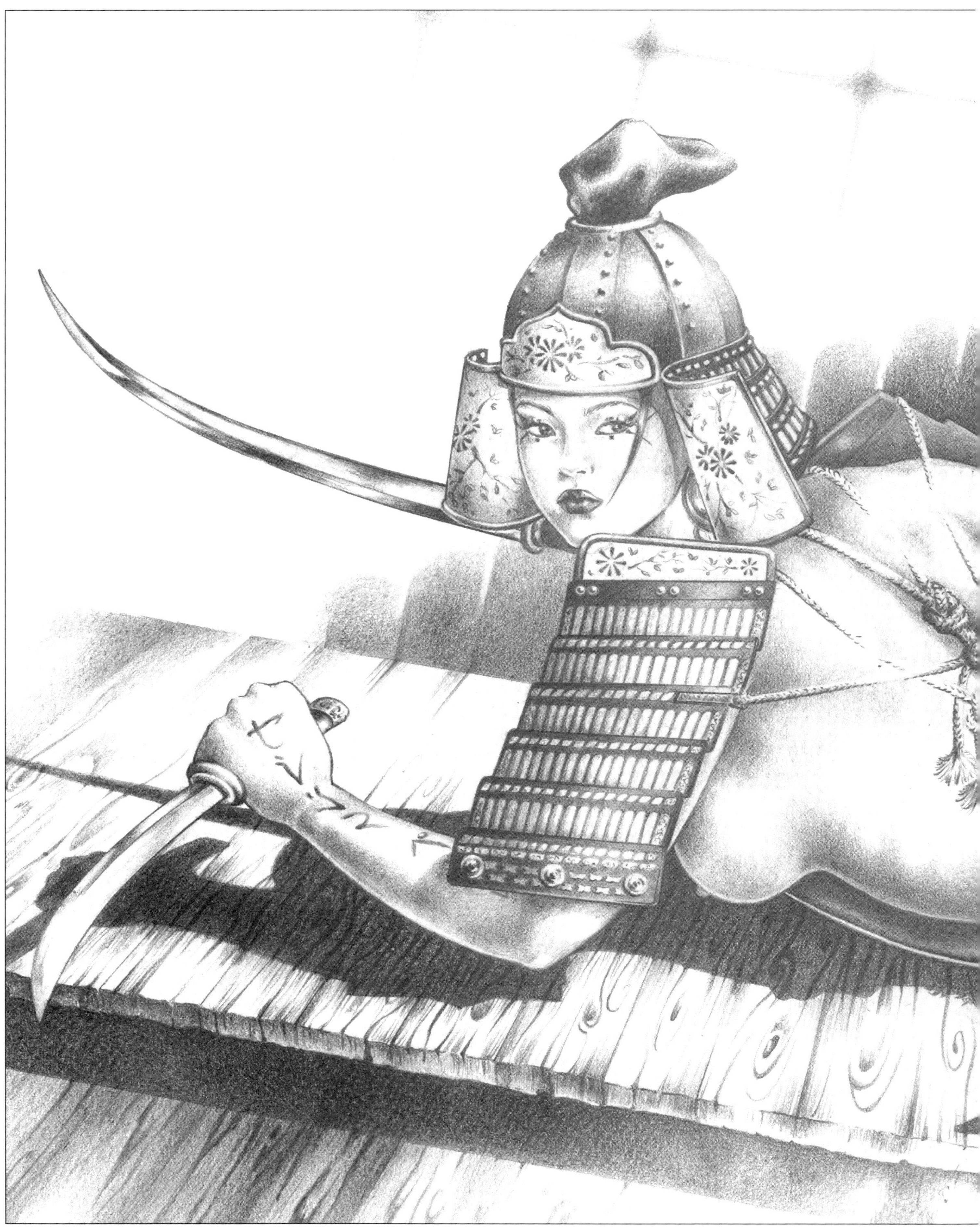

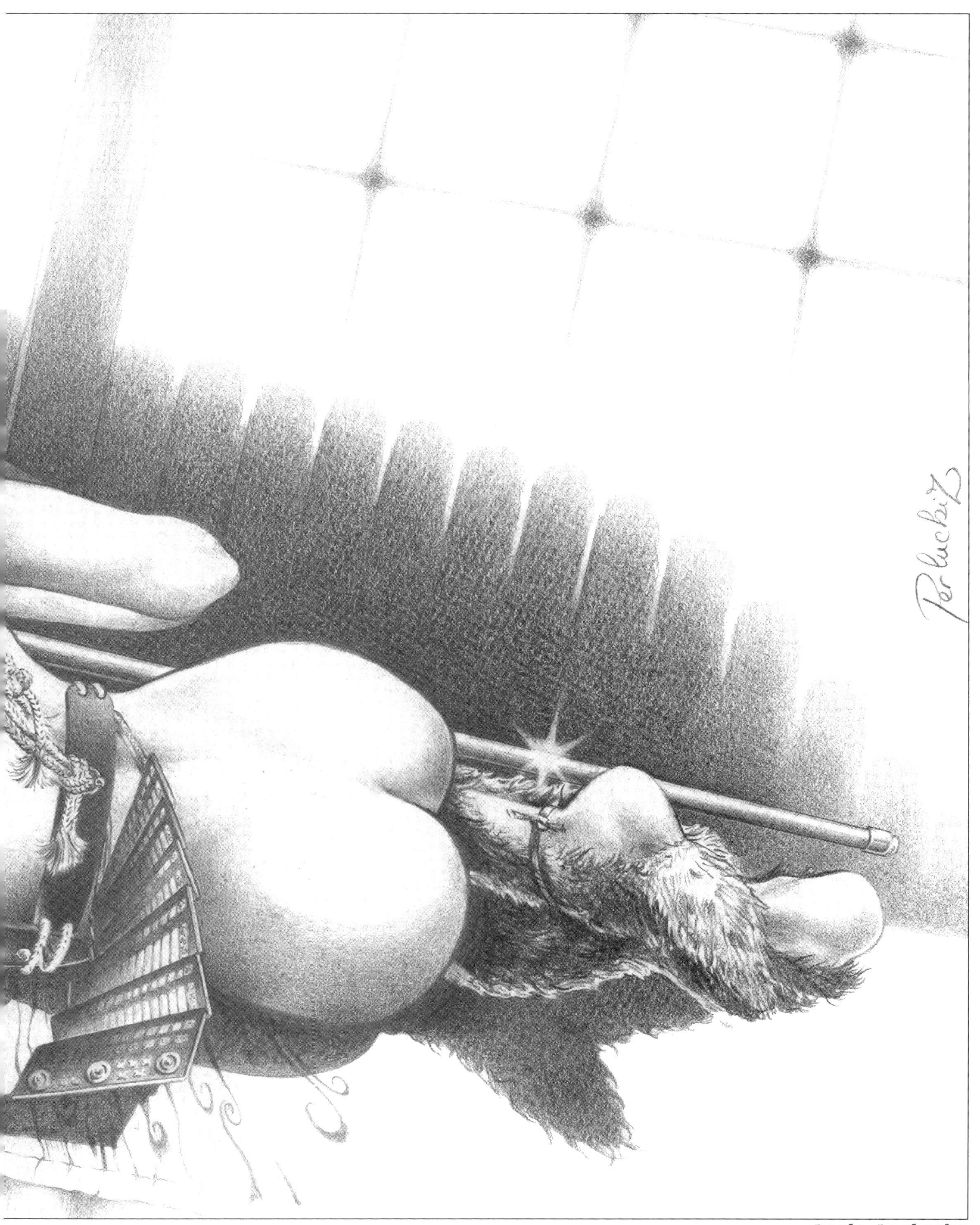

Perla Perlucky

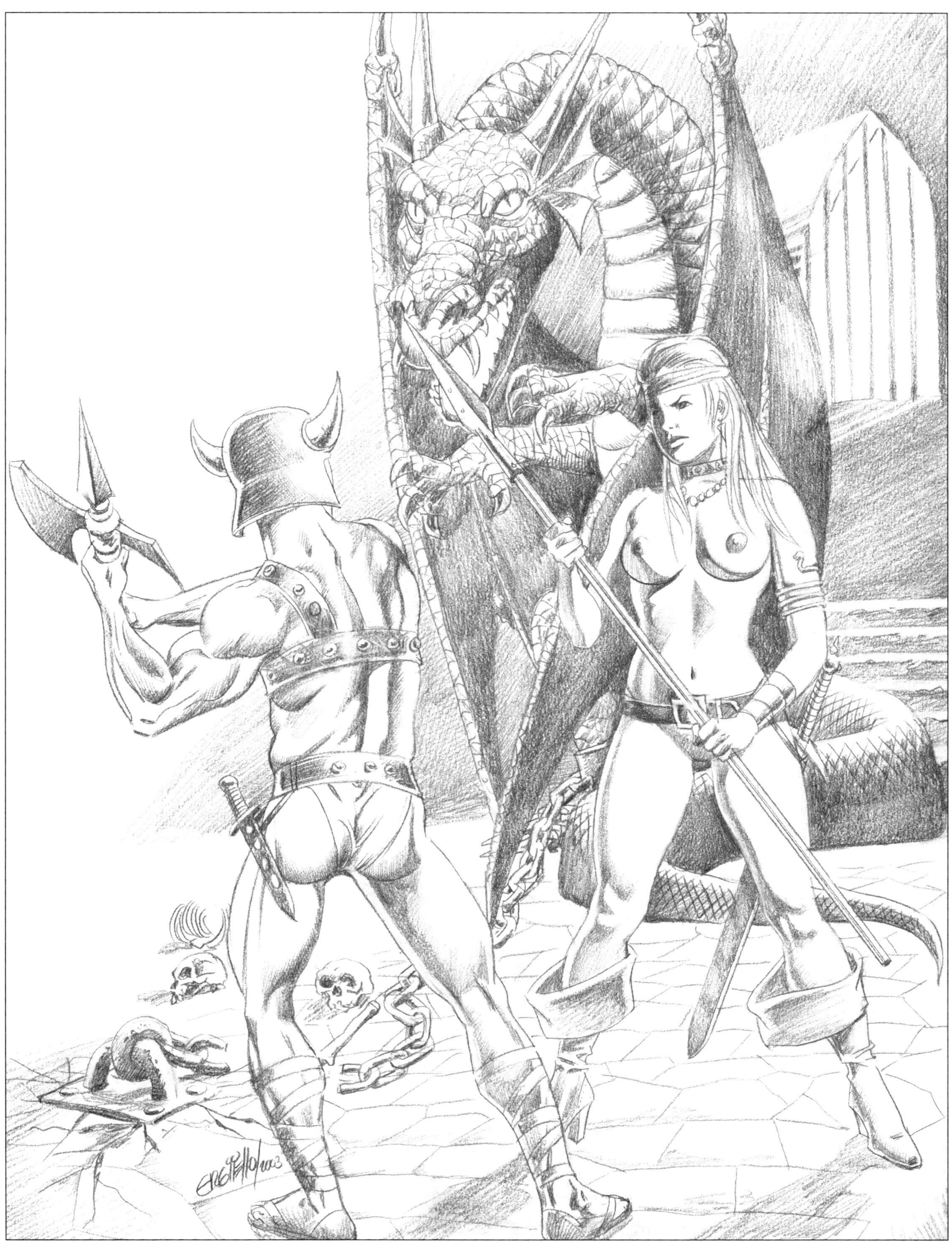

Carlos Arguello

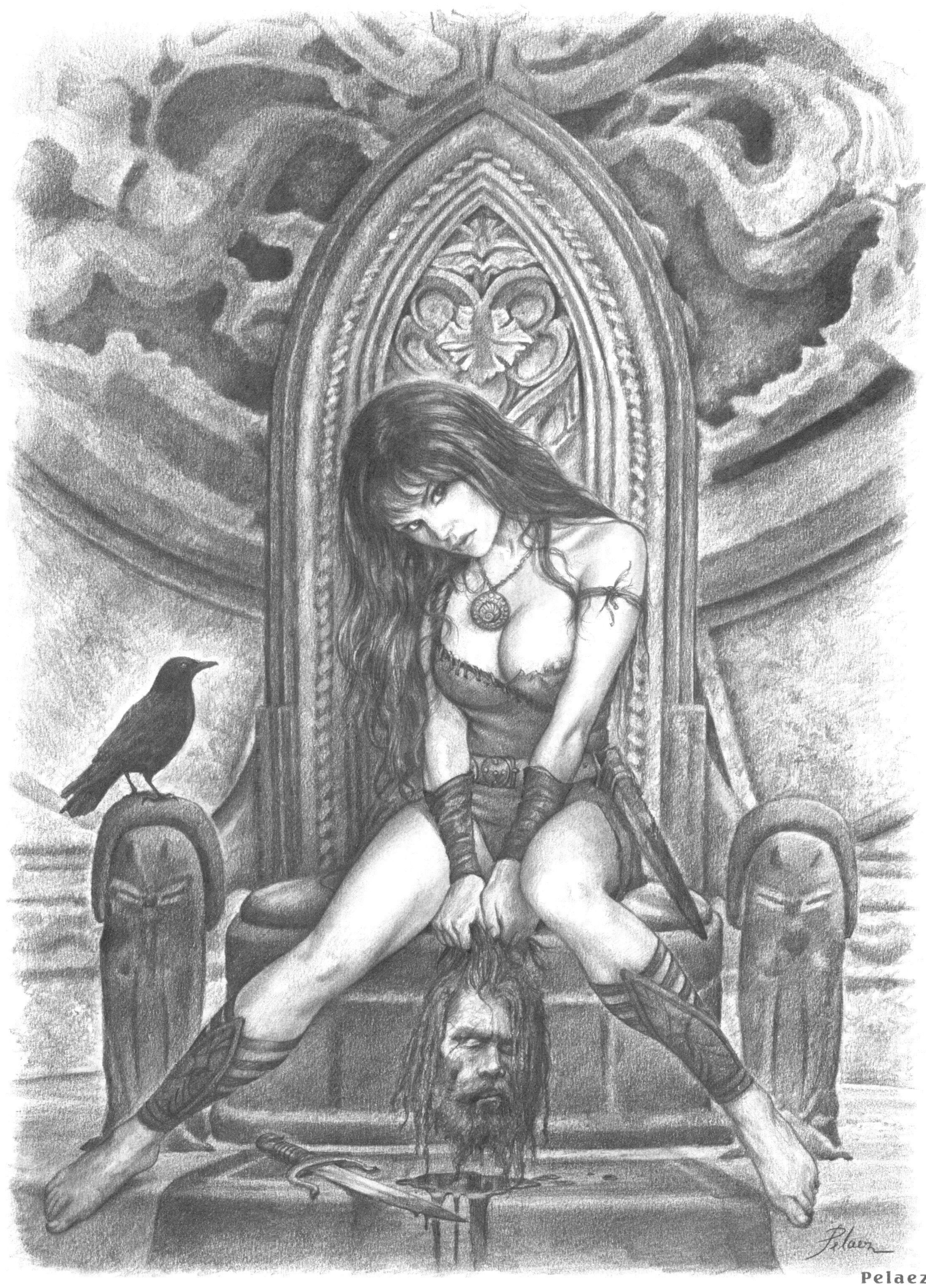

Pelaez

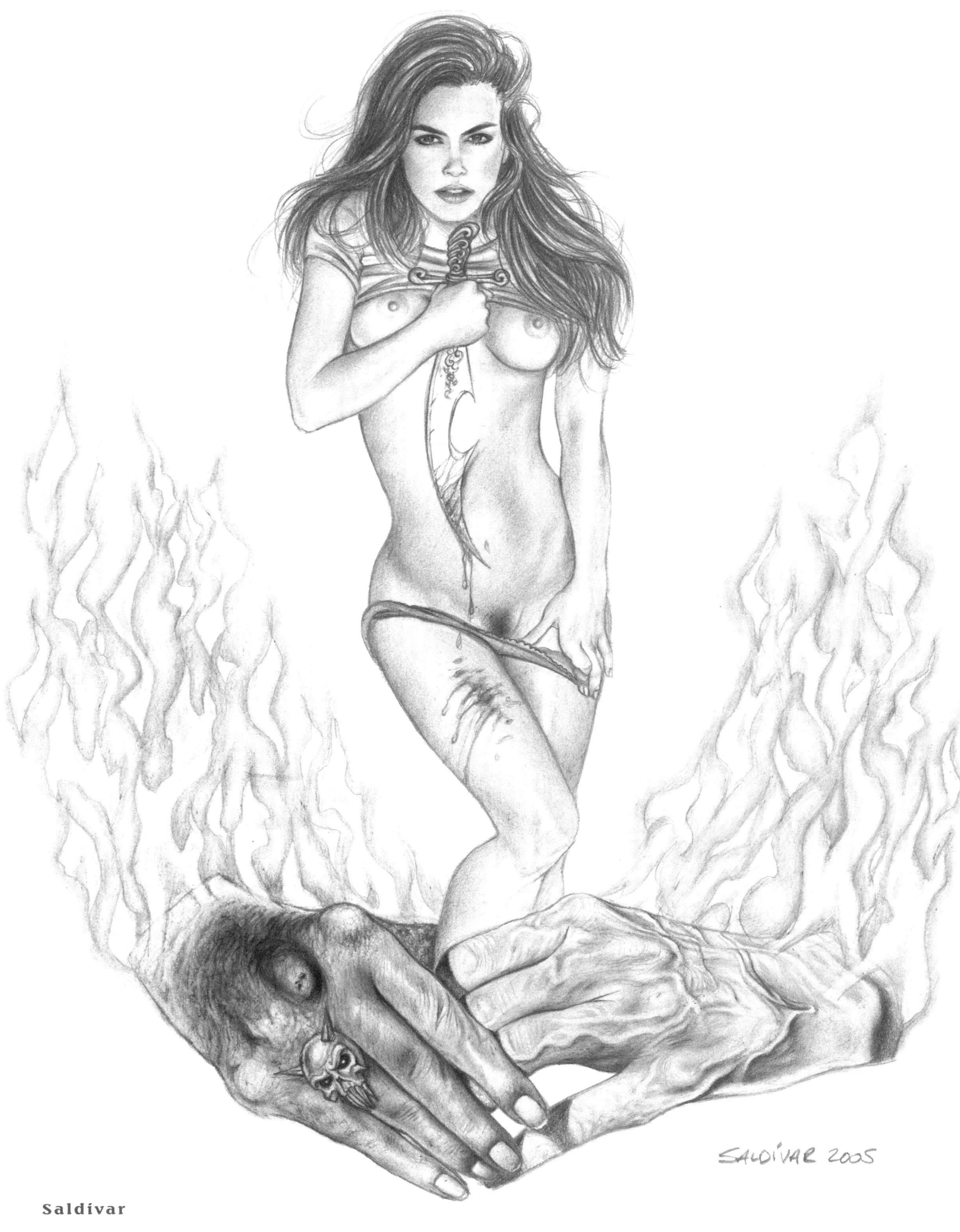

Saldívar

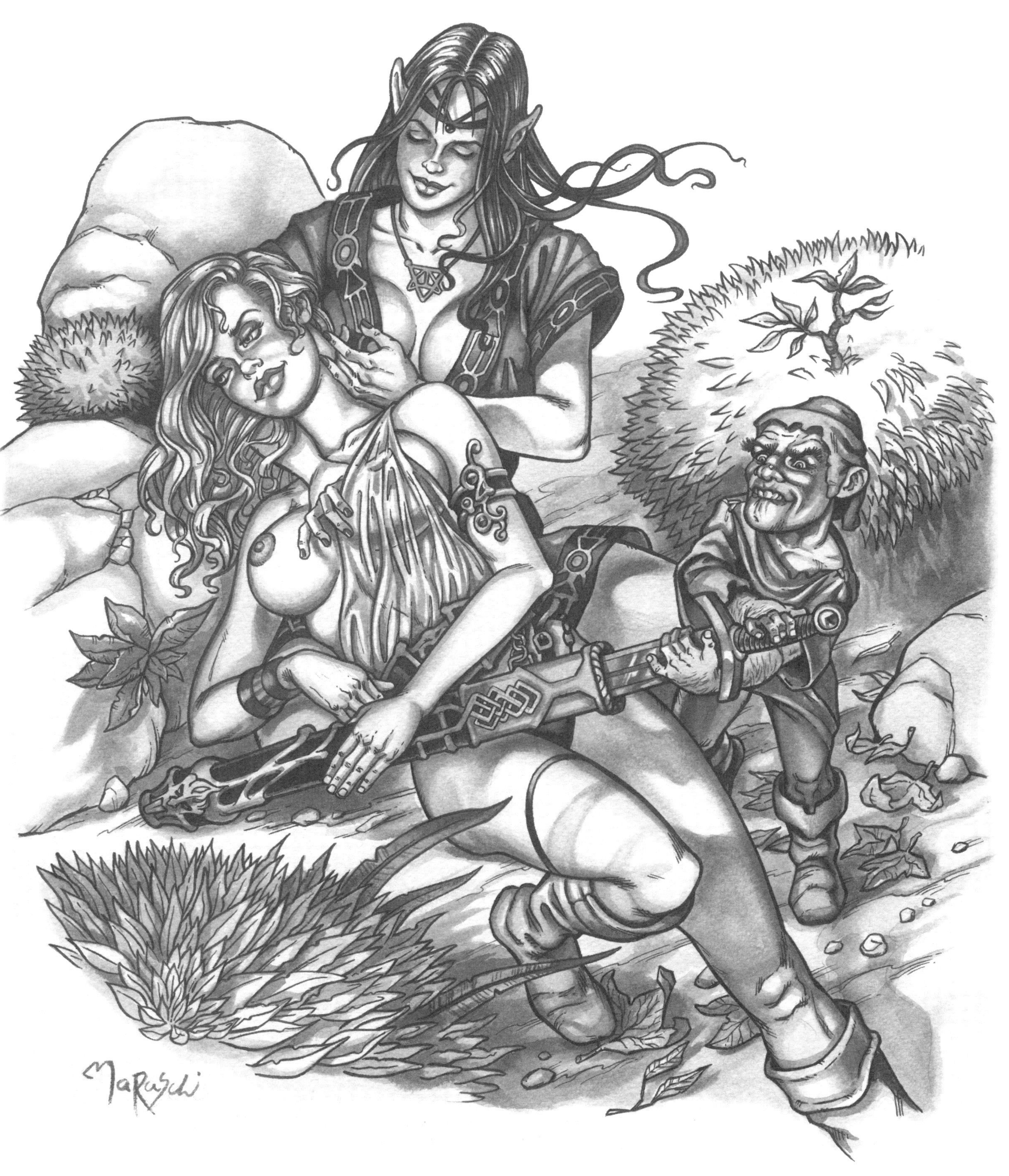

Aníbal Maraschi

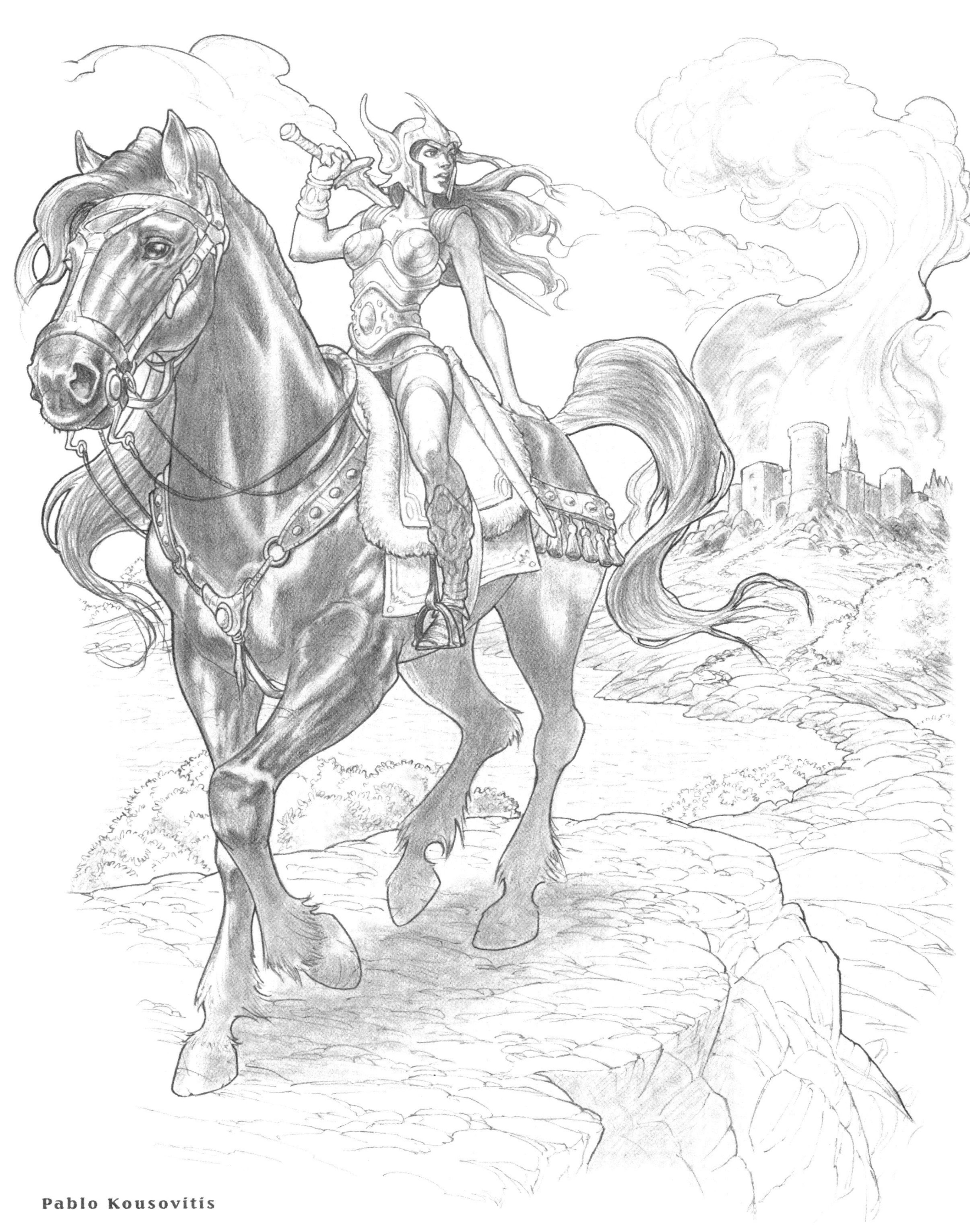

Pablo Kousovitis

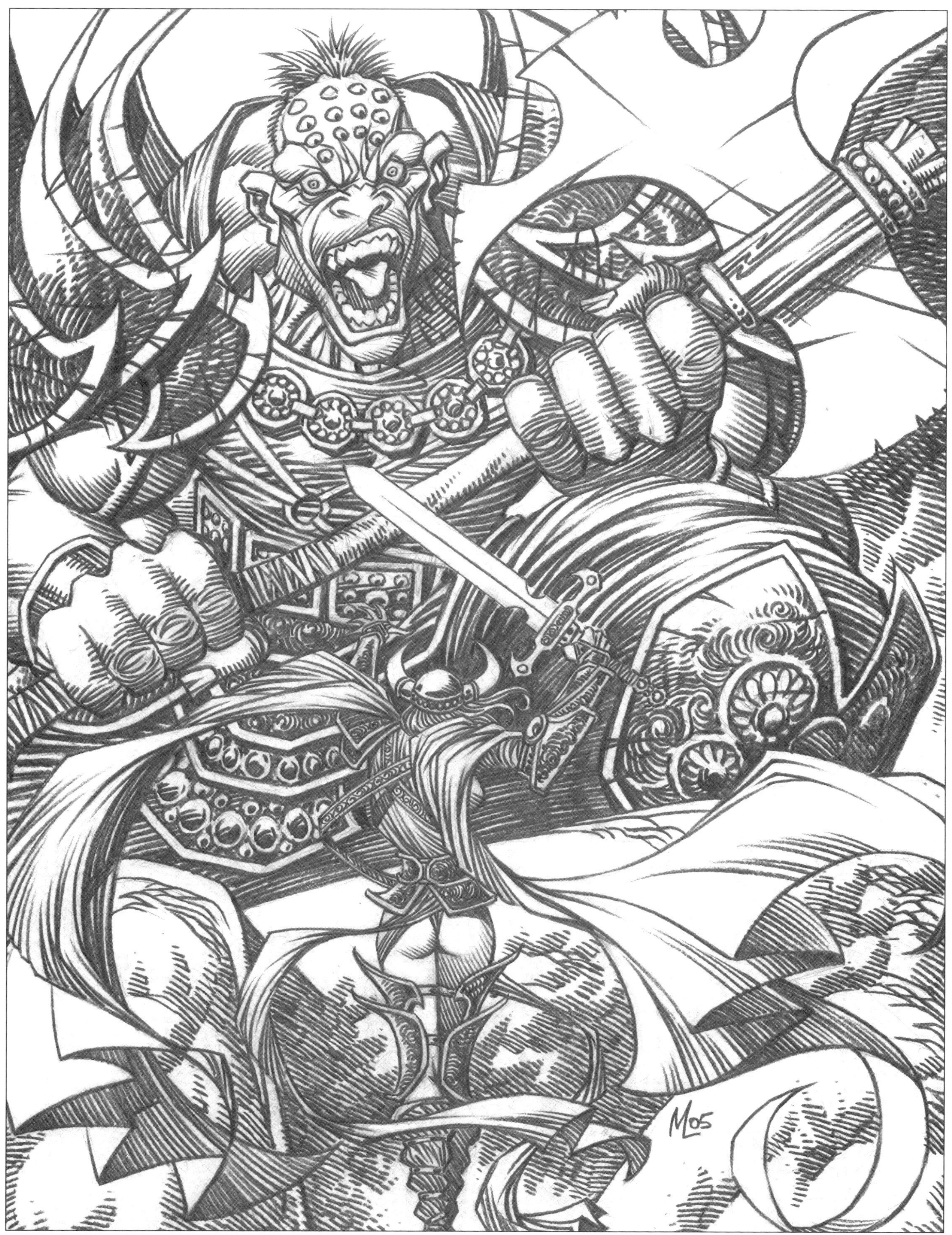

Ruben Meriggi

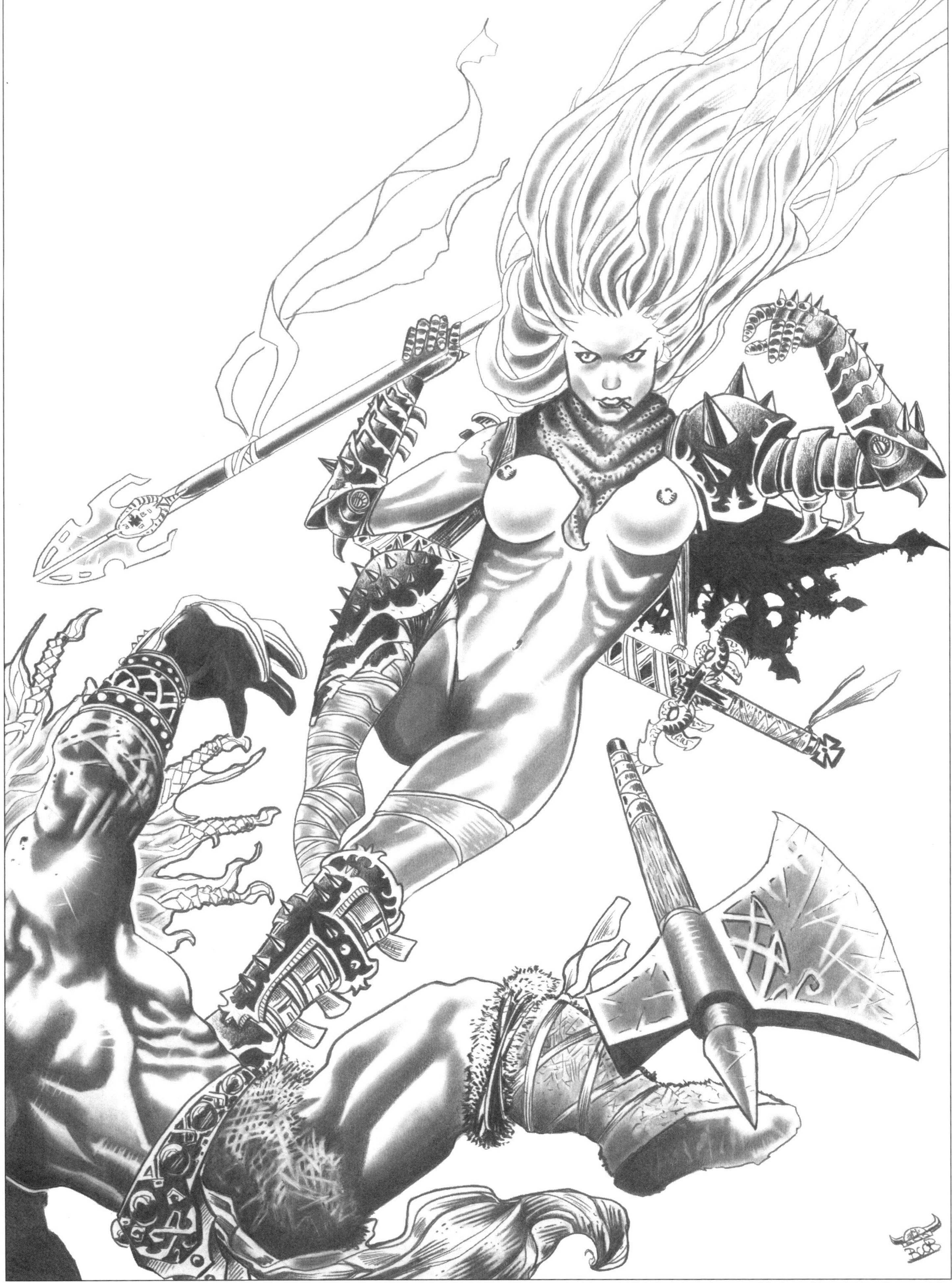

Luis Buci

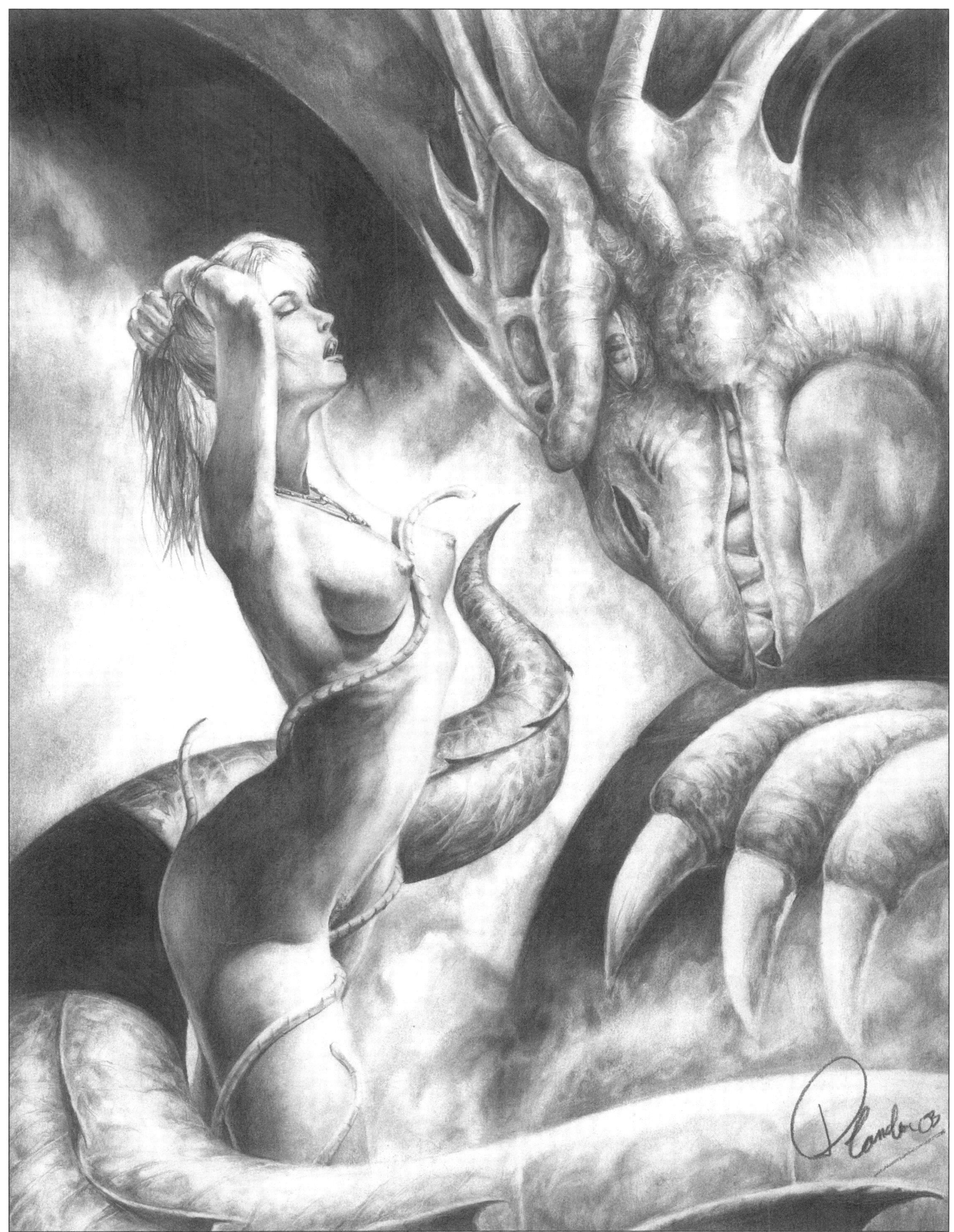

Diego Candia

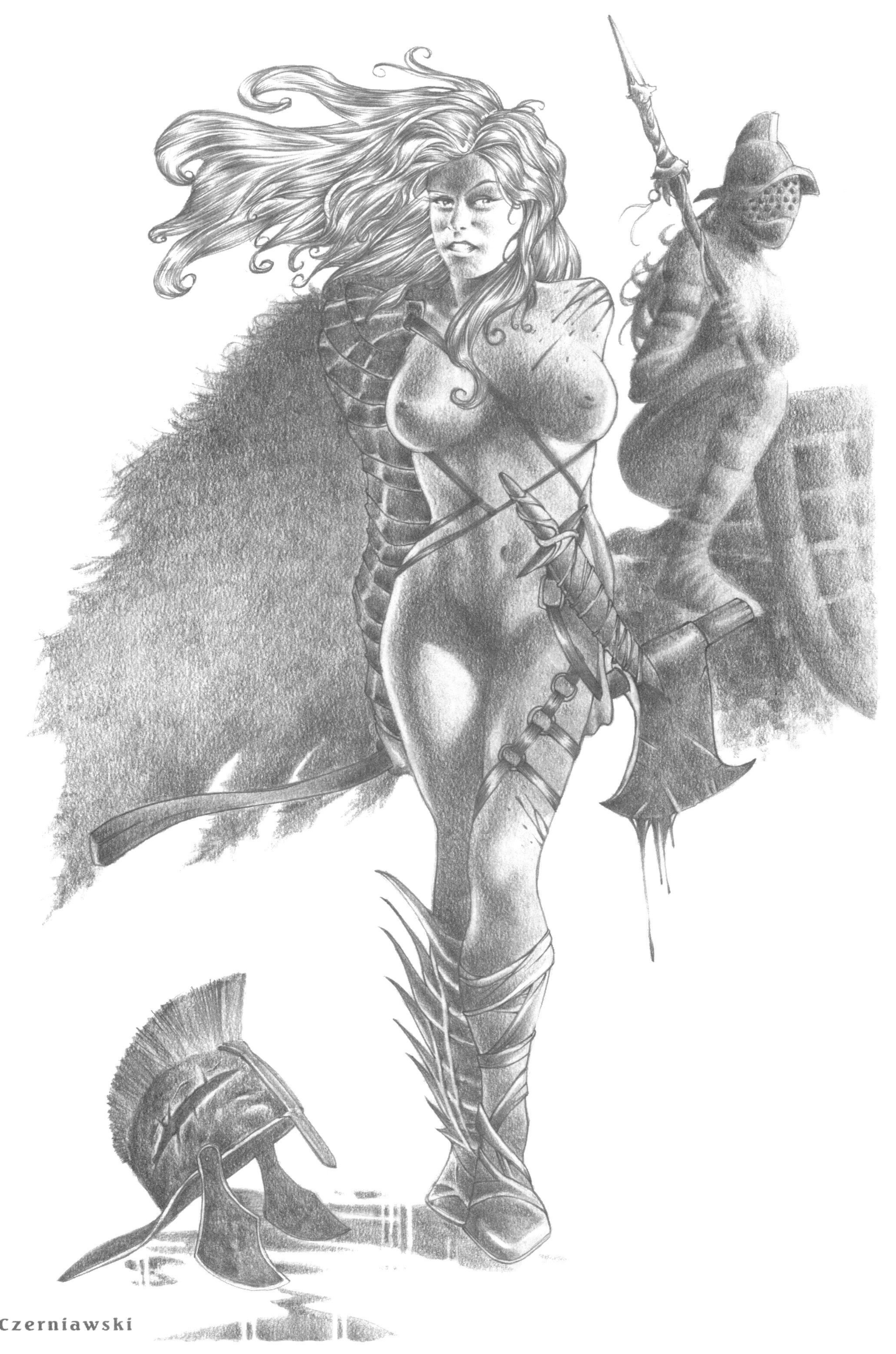
J.L. Czerniawski

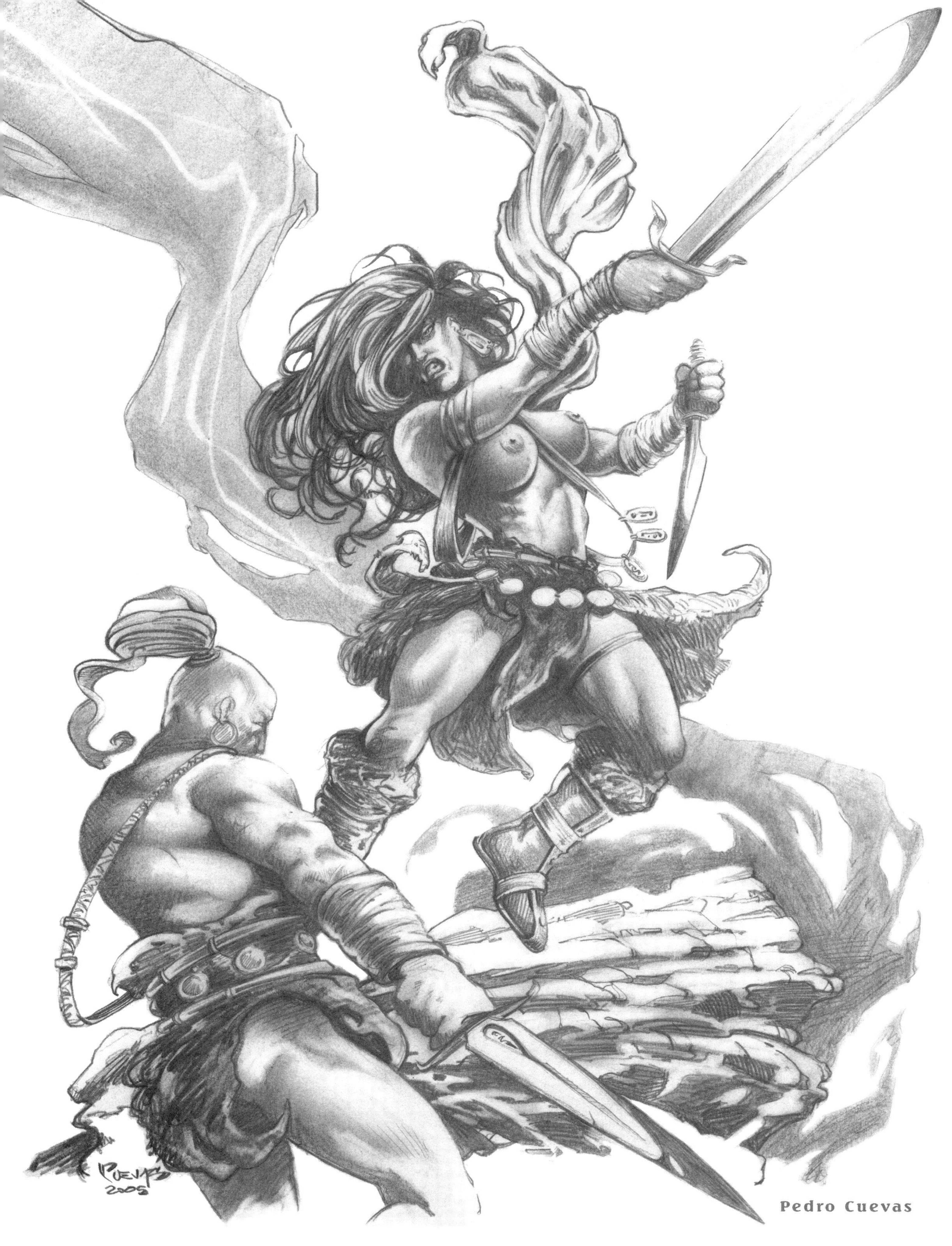

Pedro Cuevas

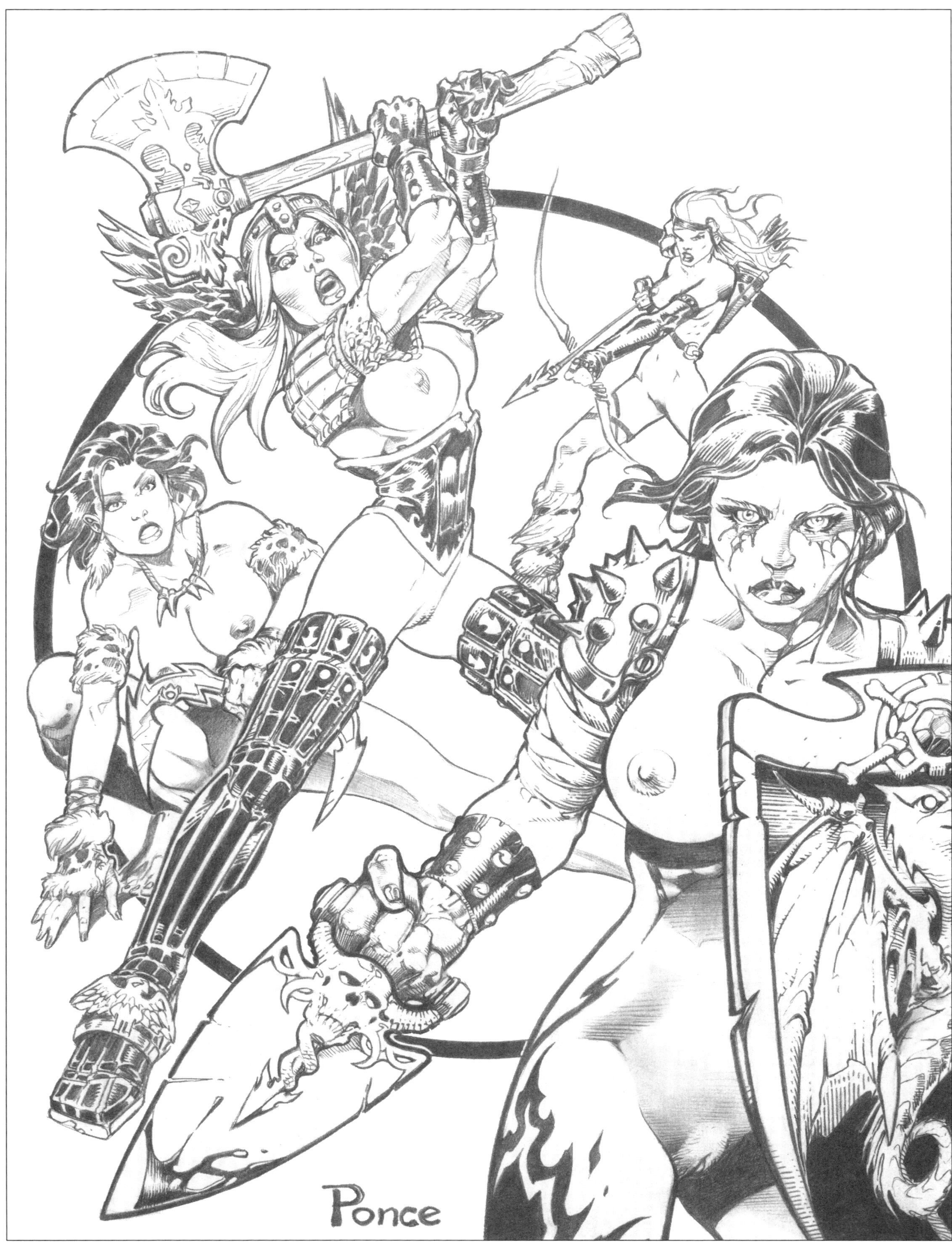

German Ponce

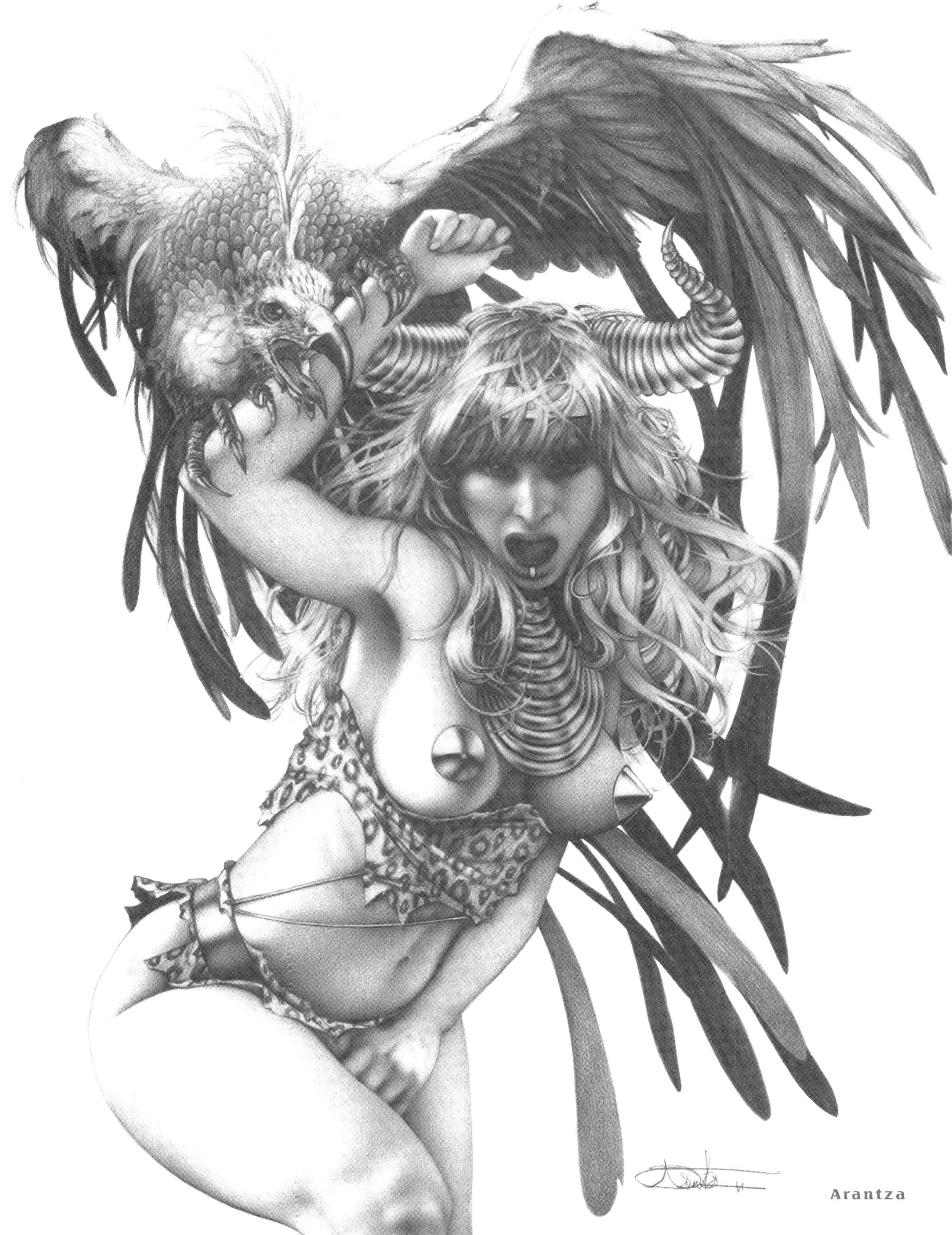

Arantza

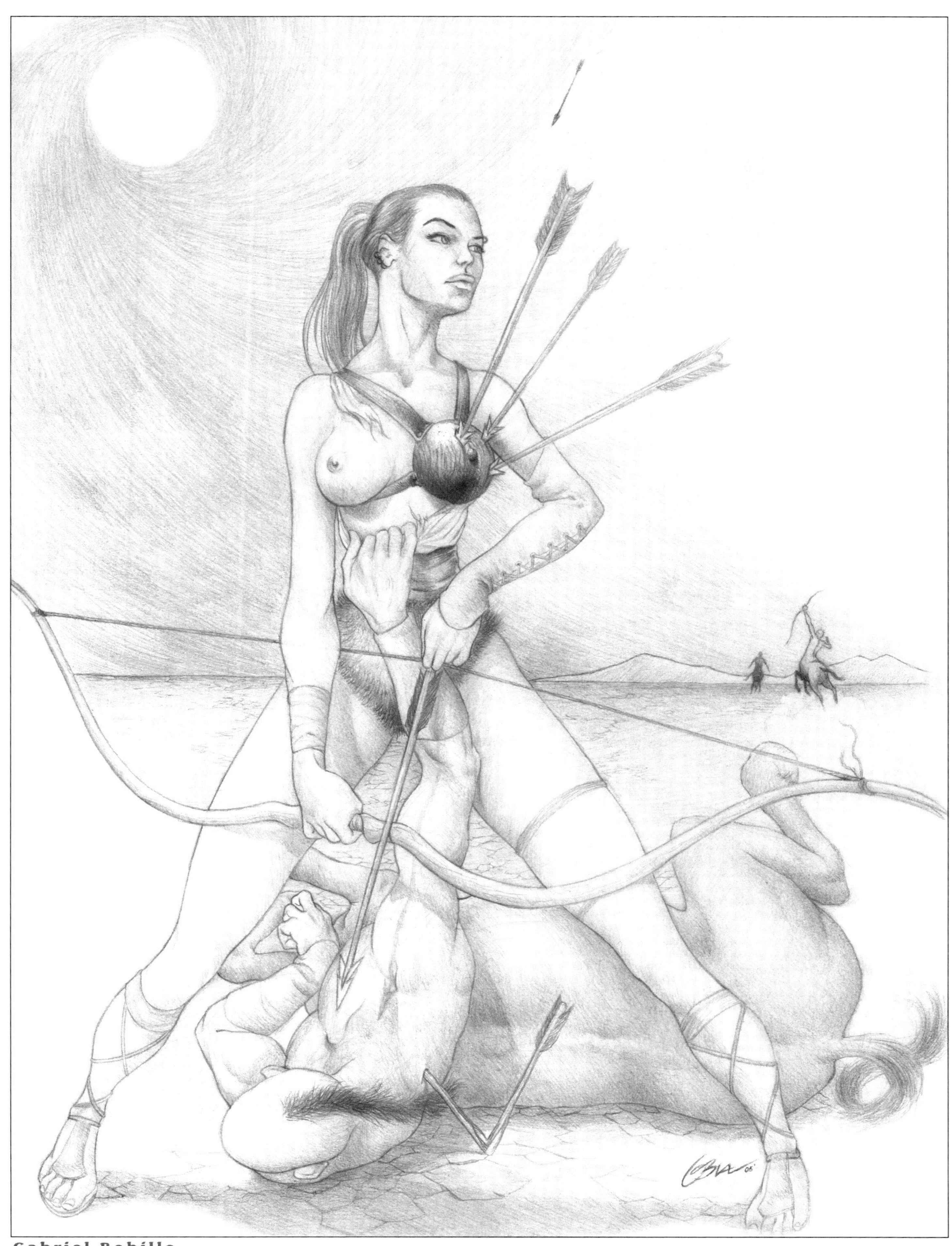

Gabriel Bobillo

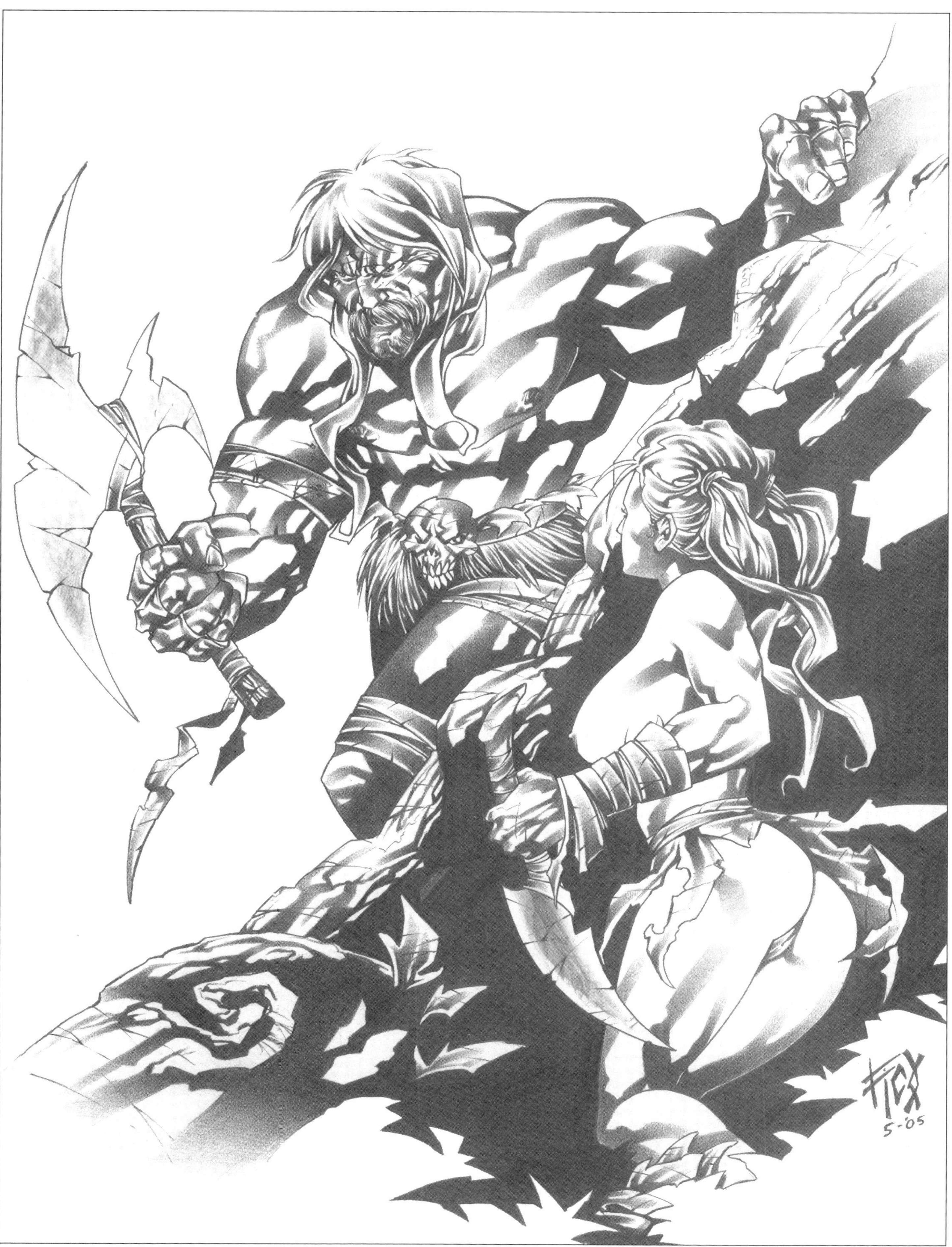

Federico Ossio

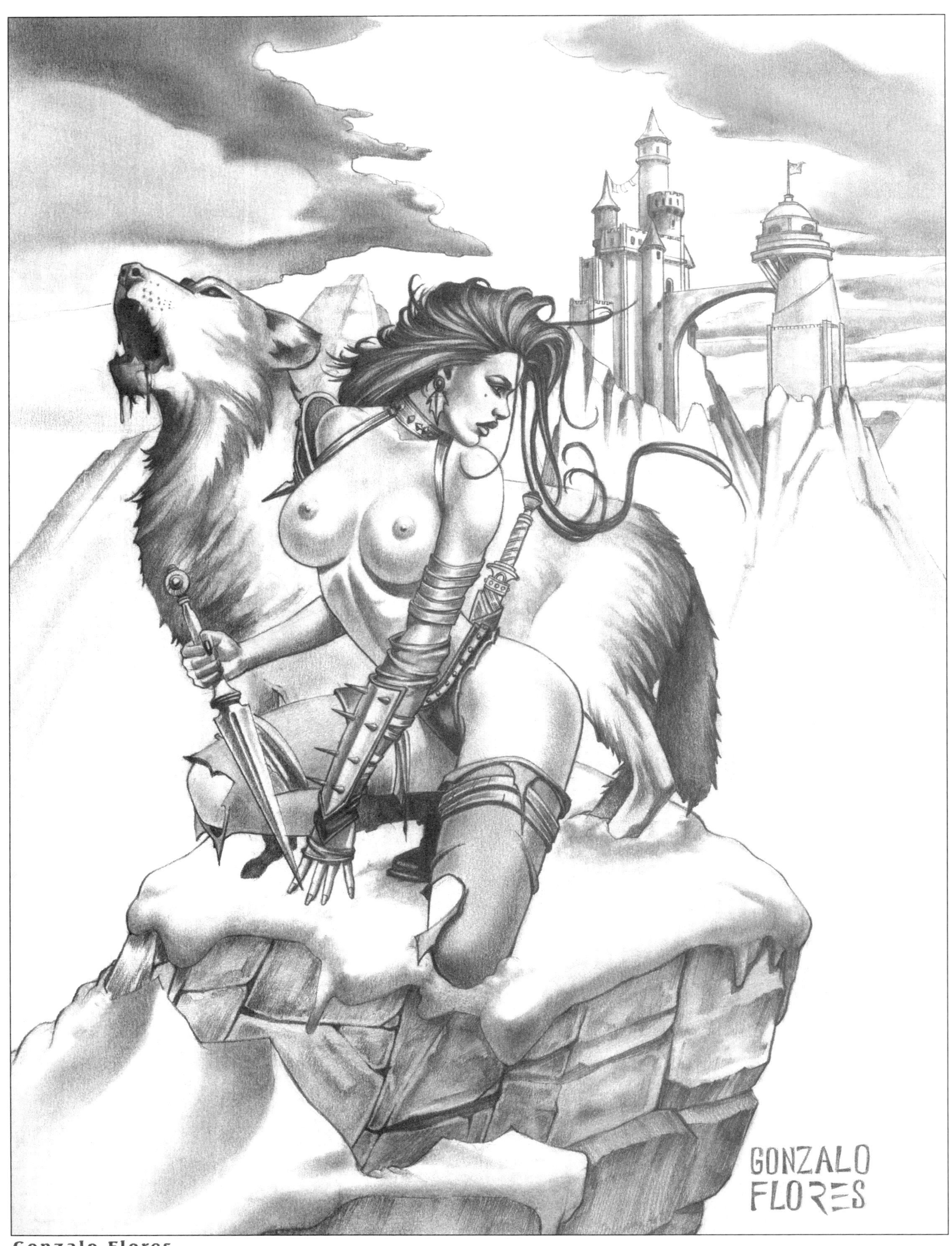

Gonzalo Flores

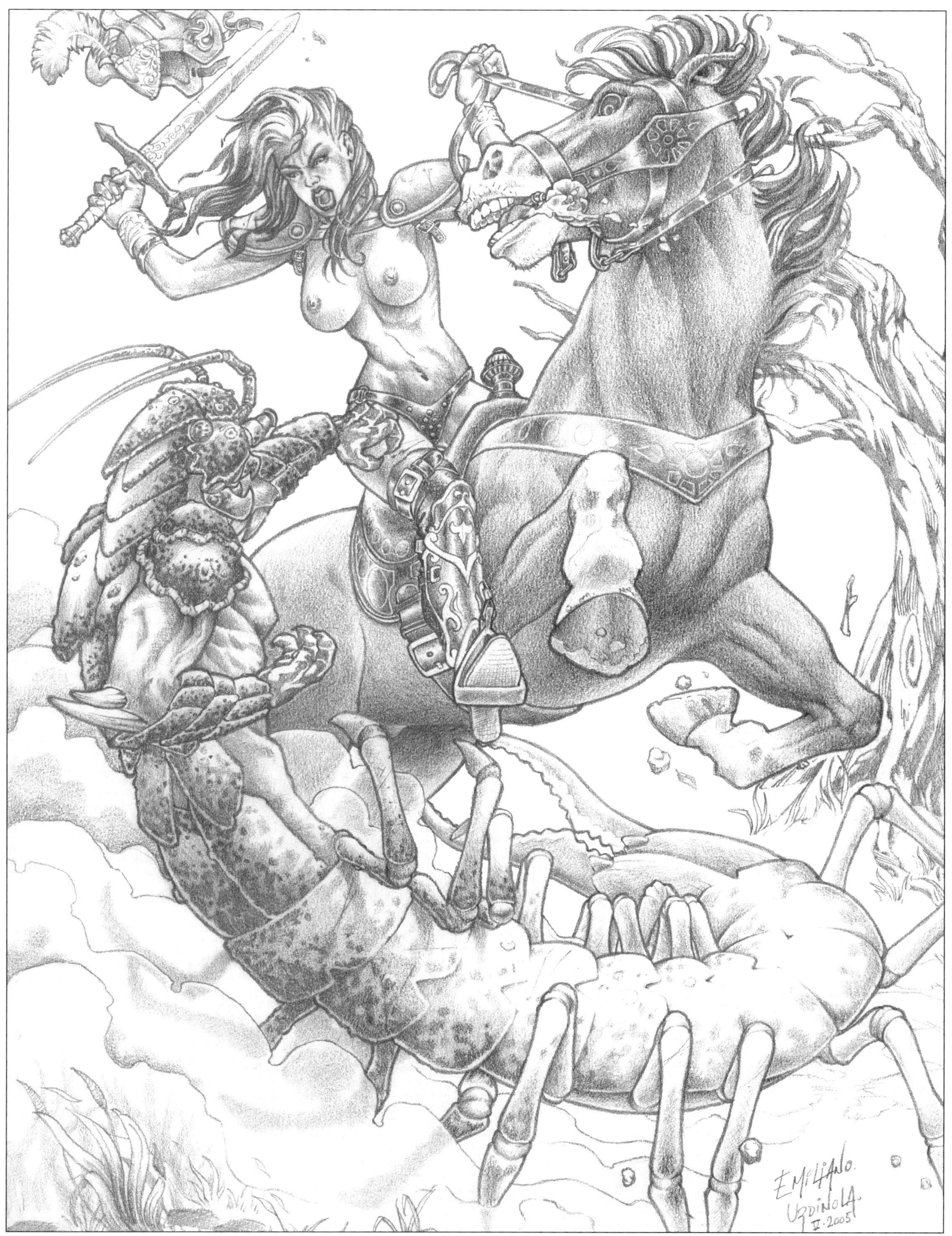

Emiliano Urdinola

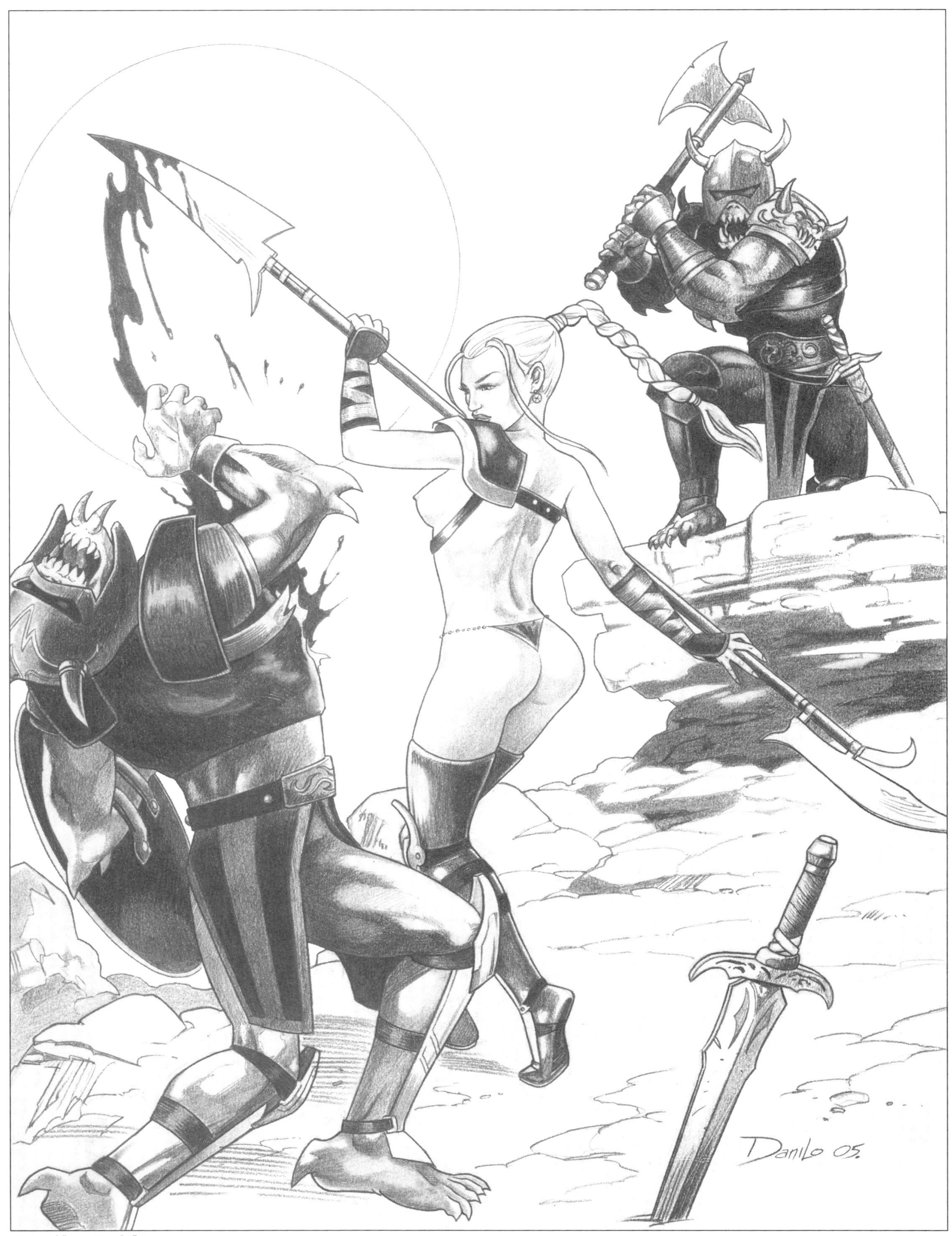

Danilo Guida

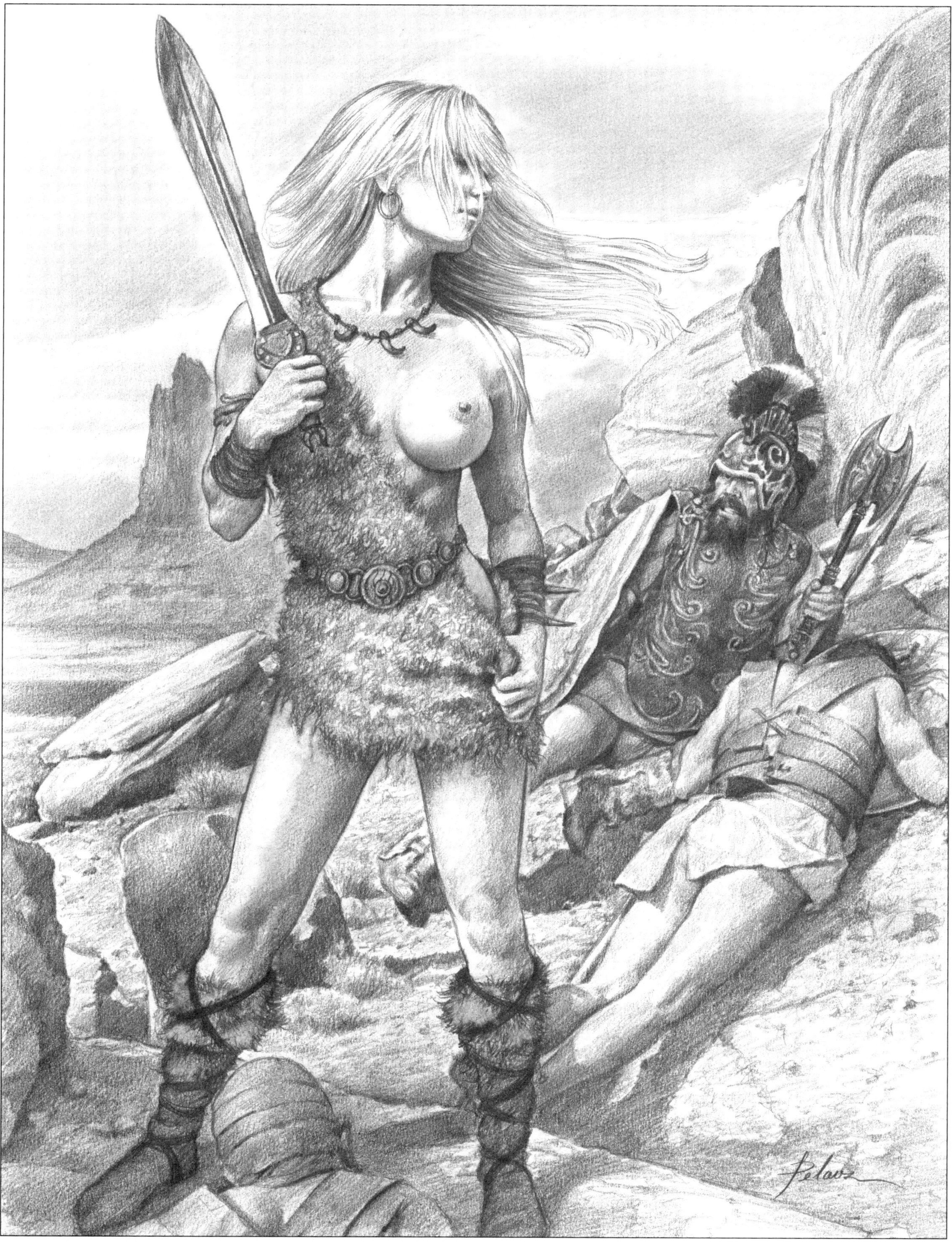

Pelaez

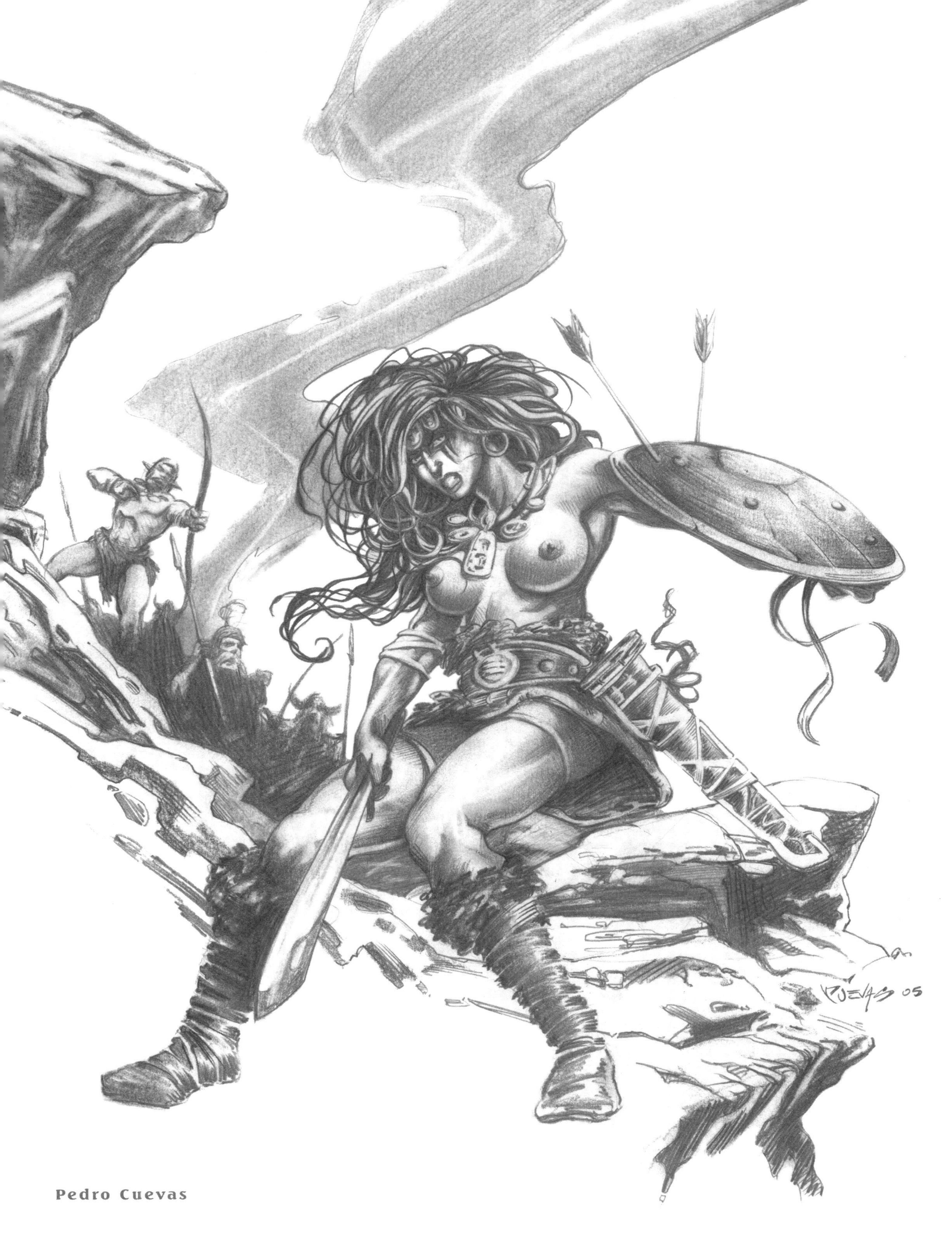

Pedro Cuevas

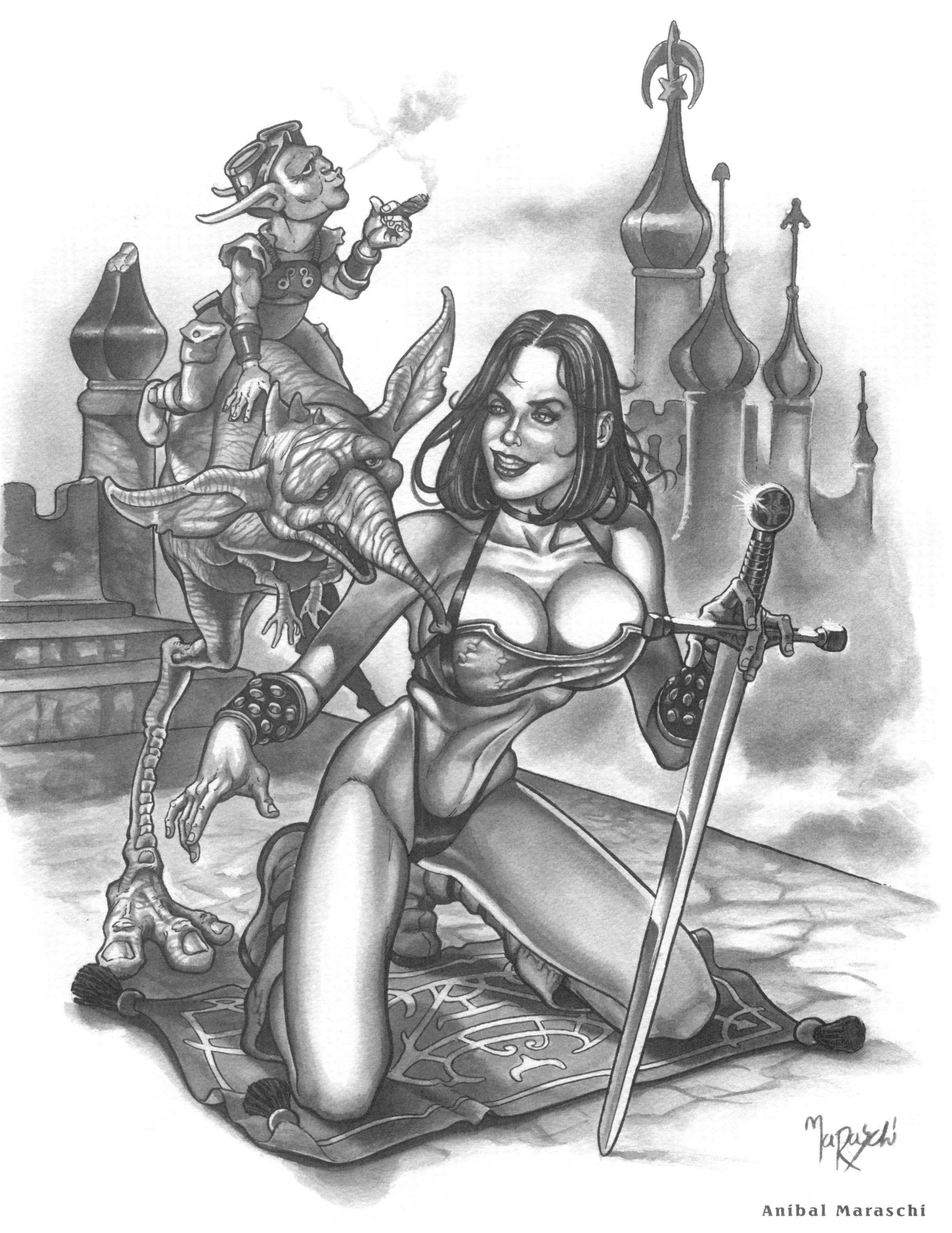

Aníbal Maraschi

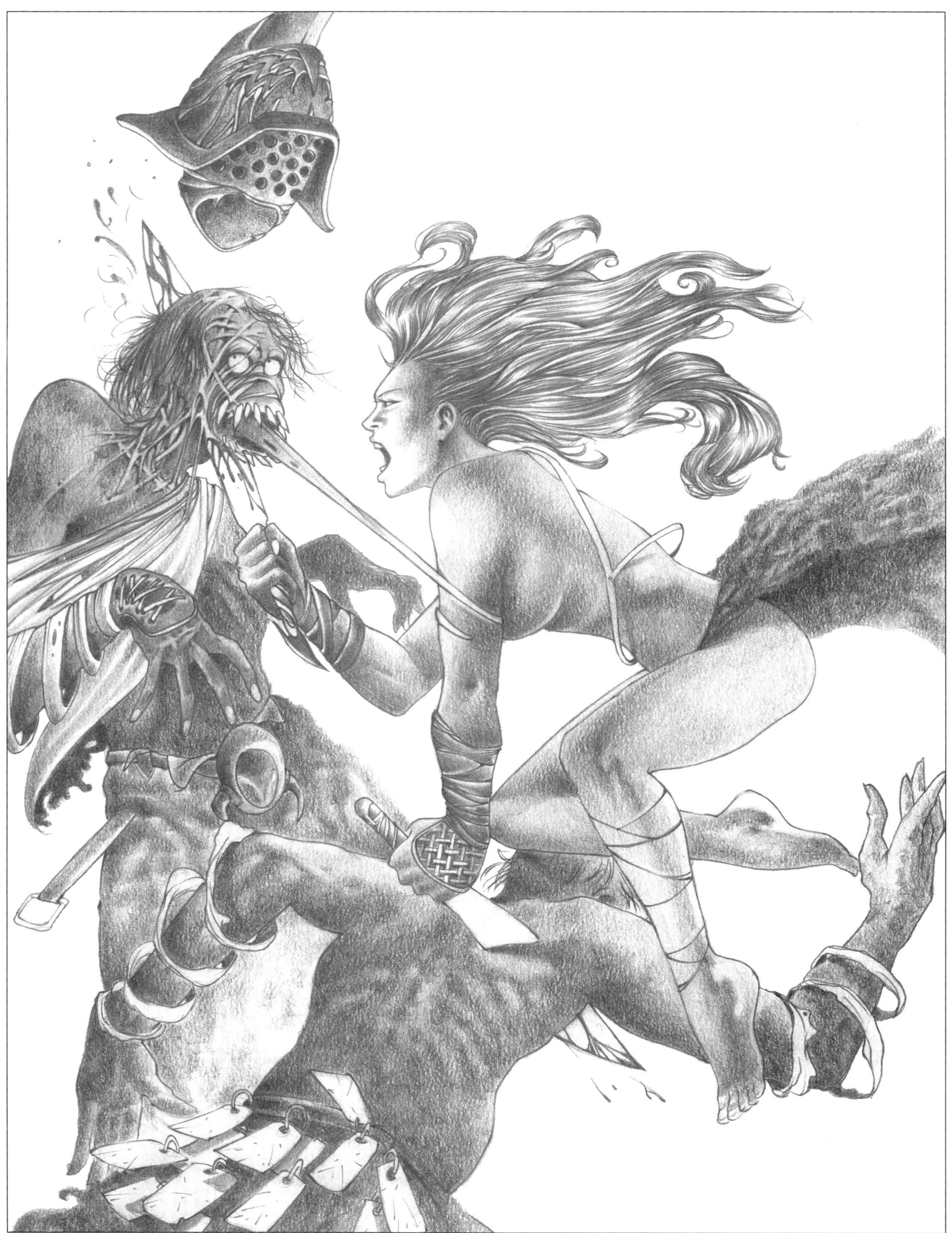

J.L. Czerniawski

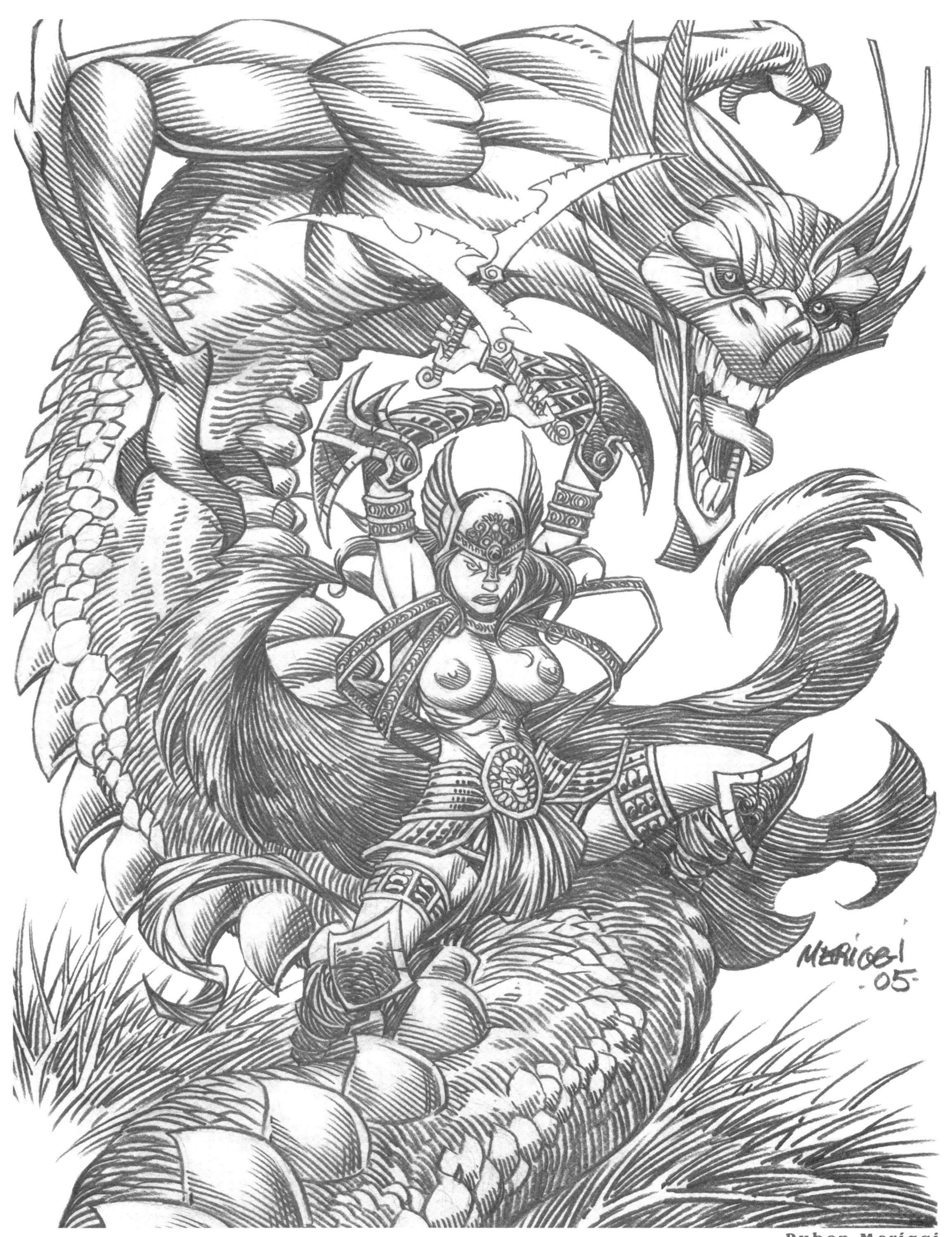

Ruben Meriggi

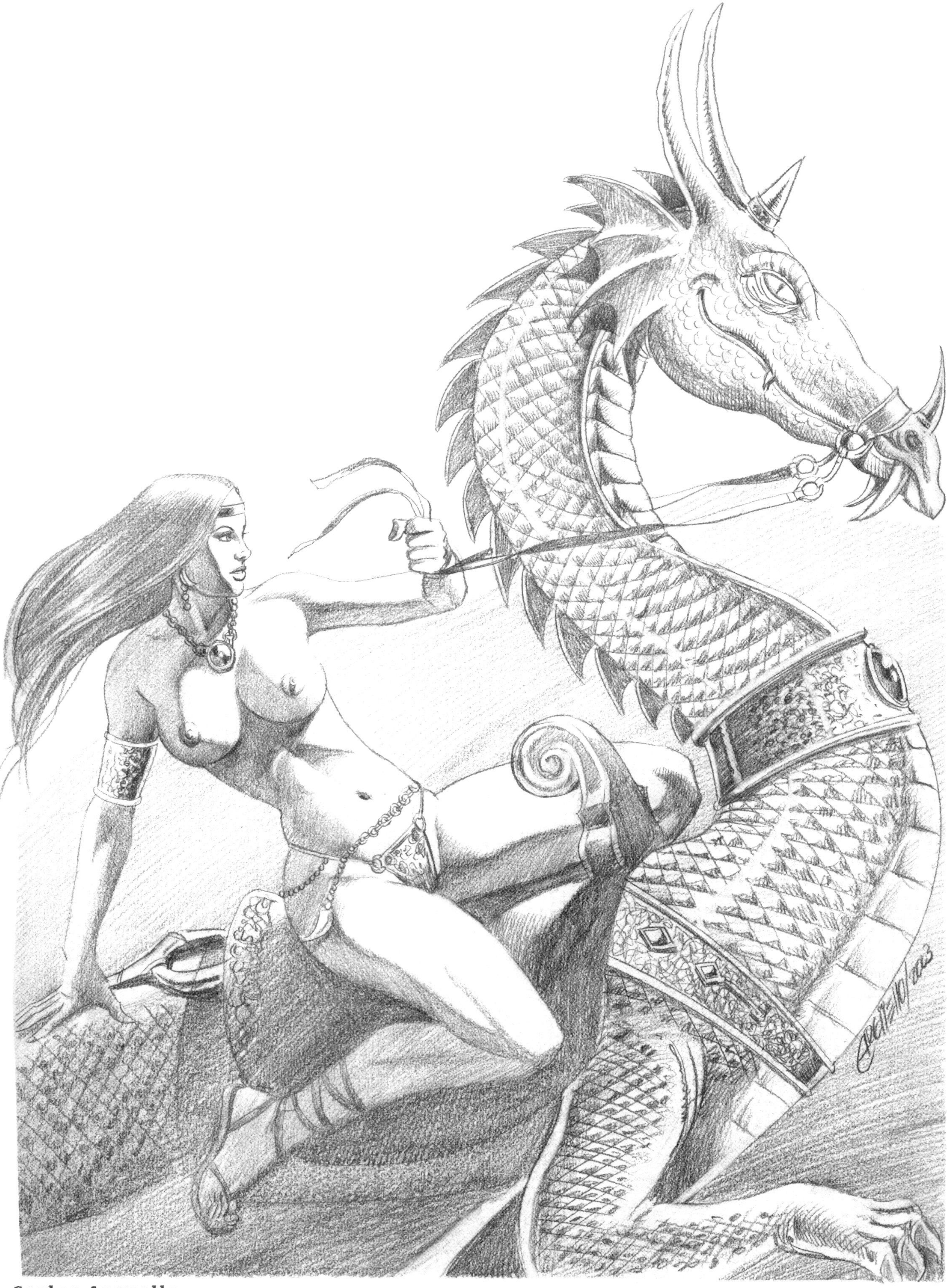

Carlos Arguello

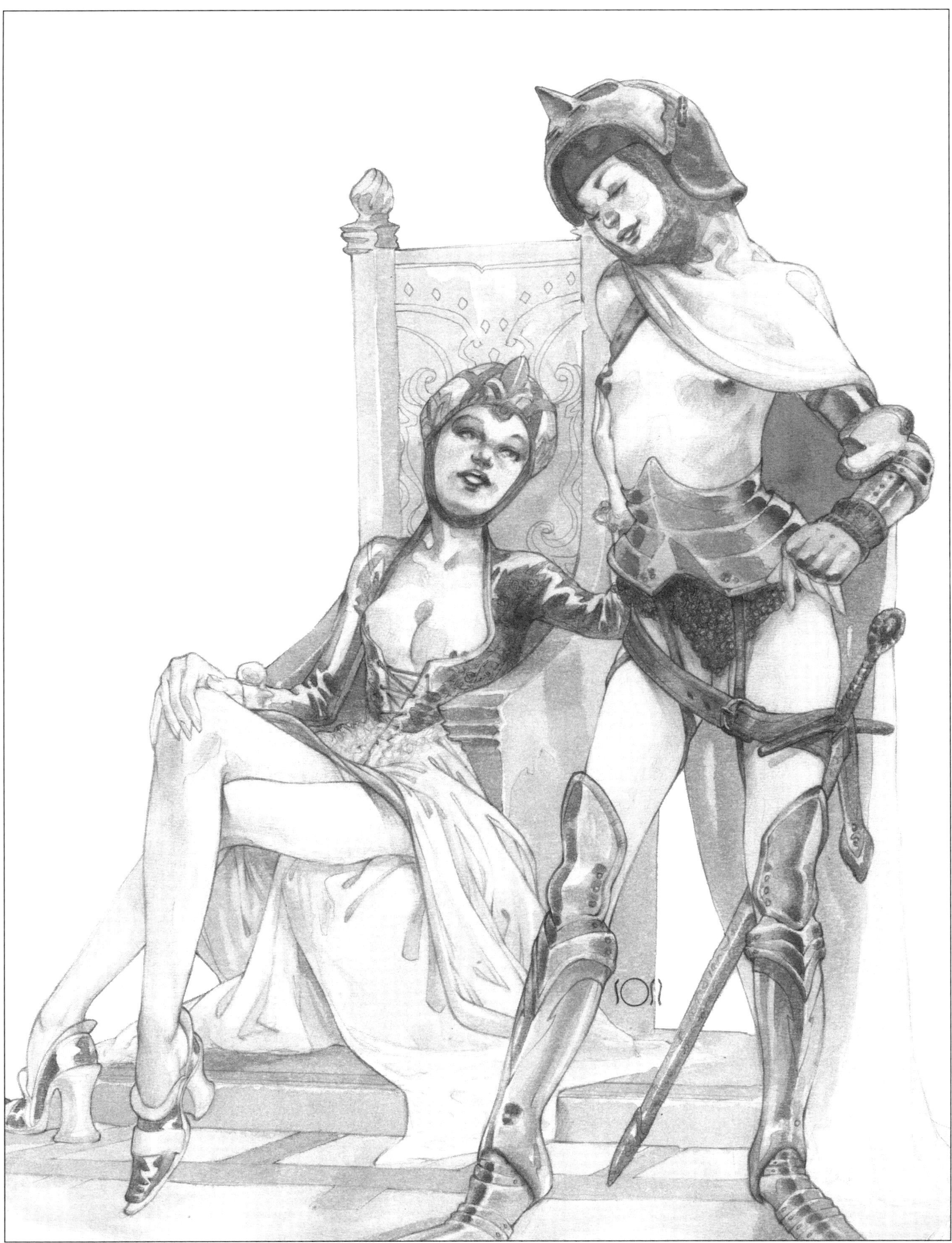

Marcelo Sosa

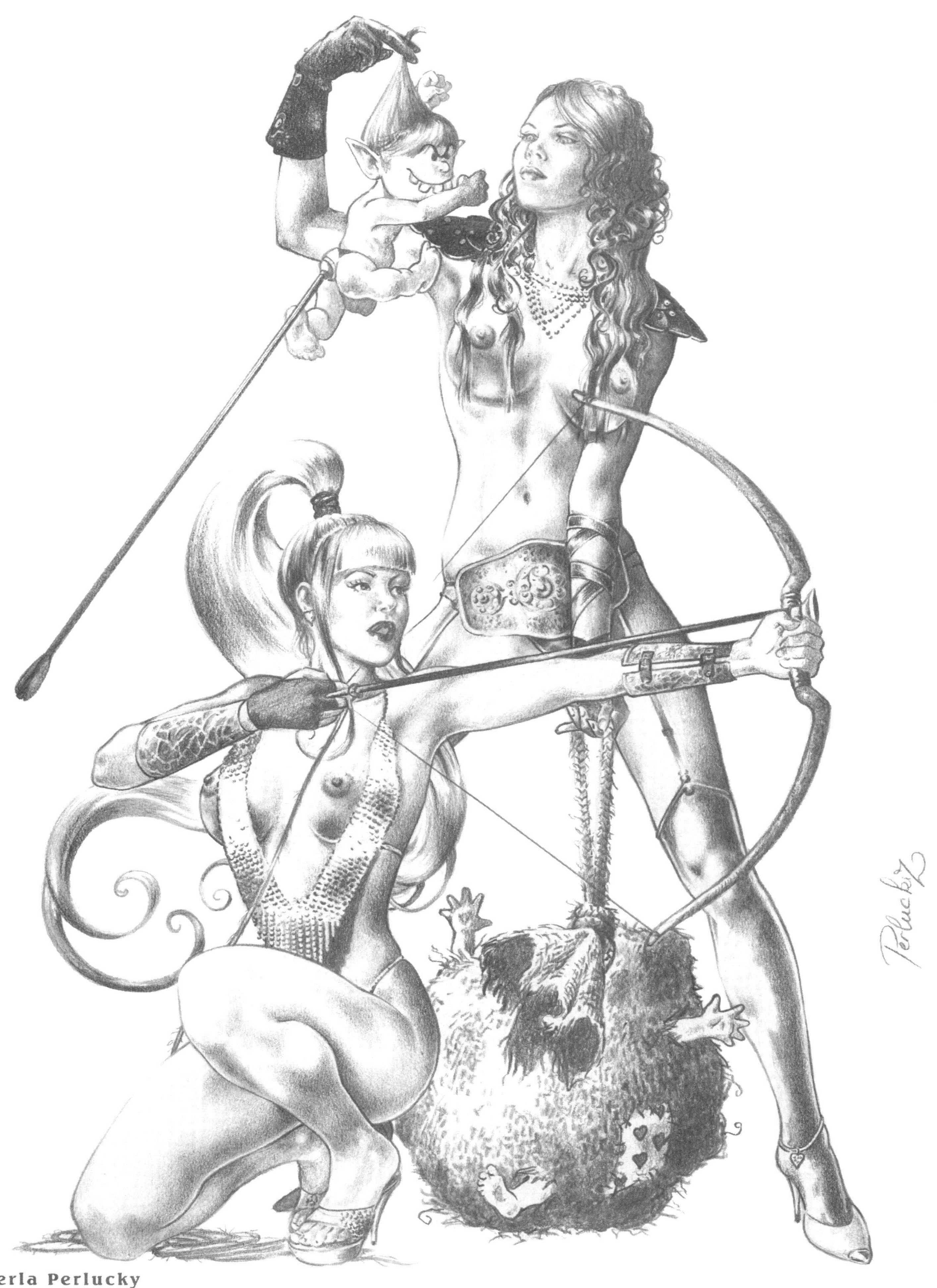

Perla Perlucky

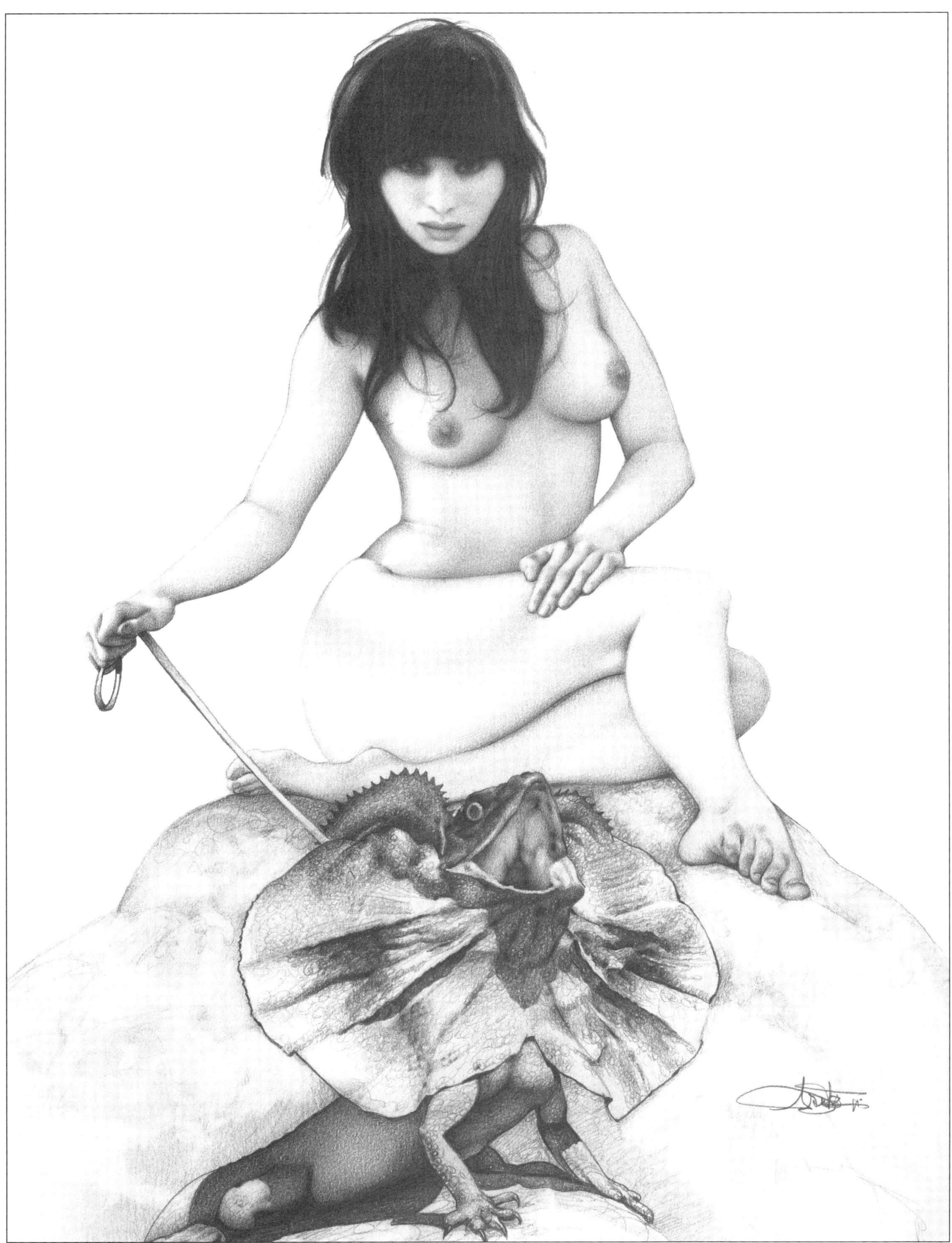

Arantza

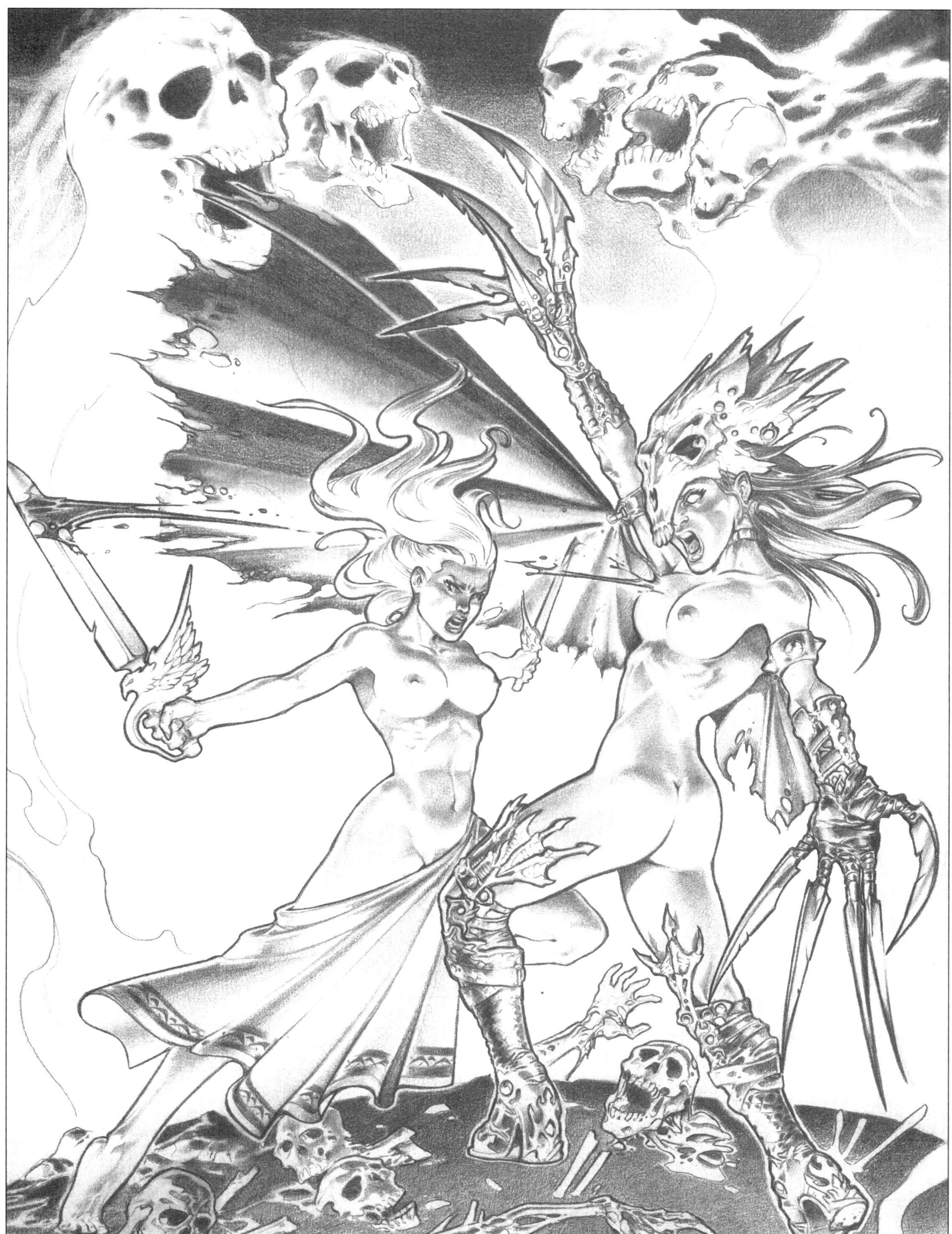

German Ponce

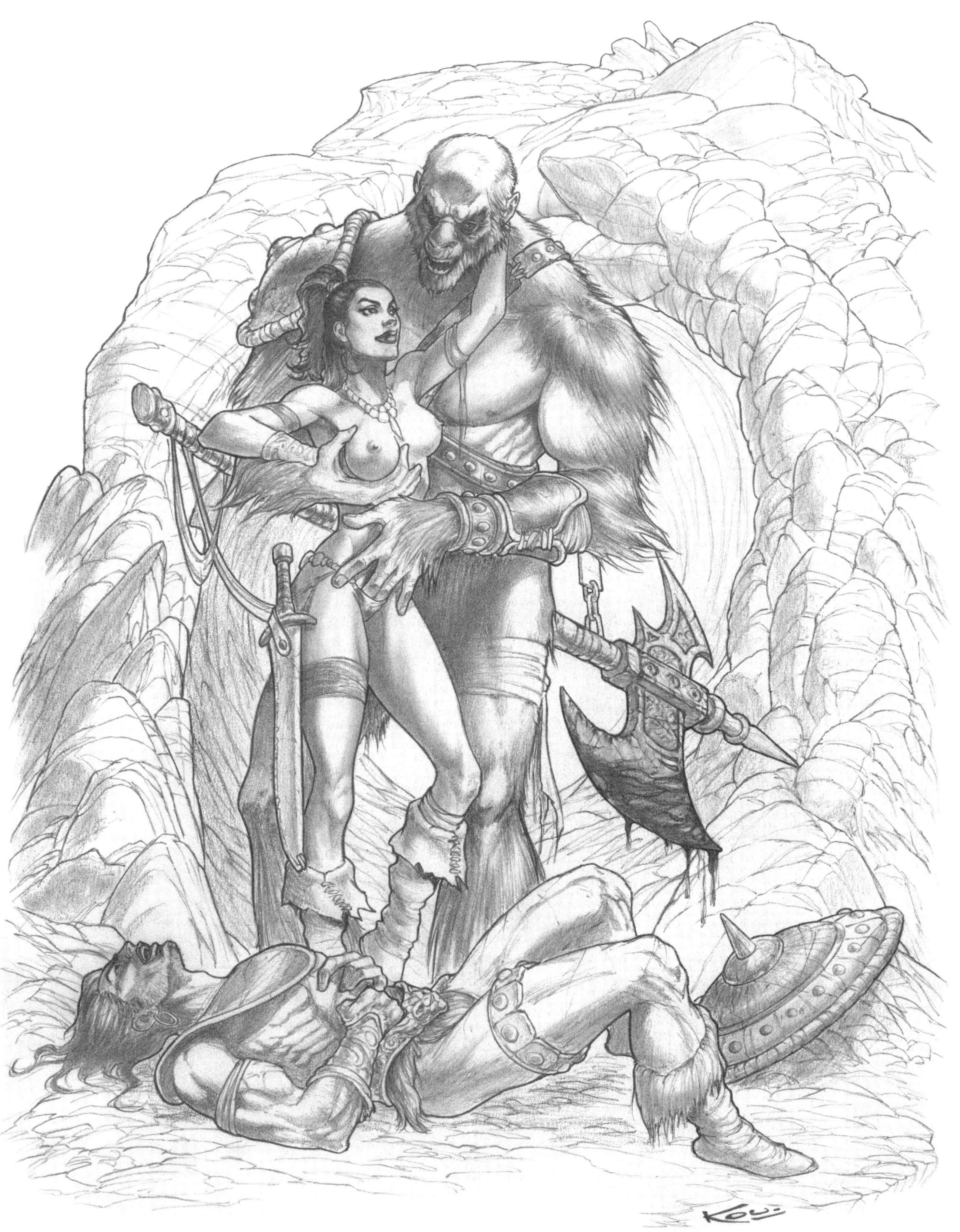

Pablo Kousovitis

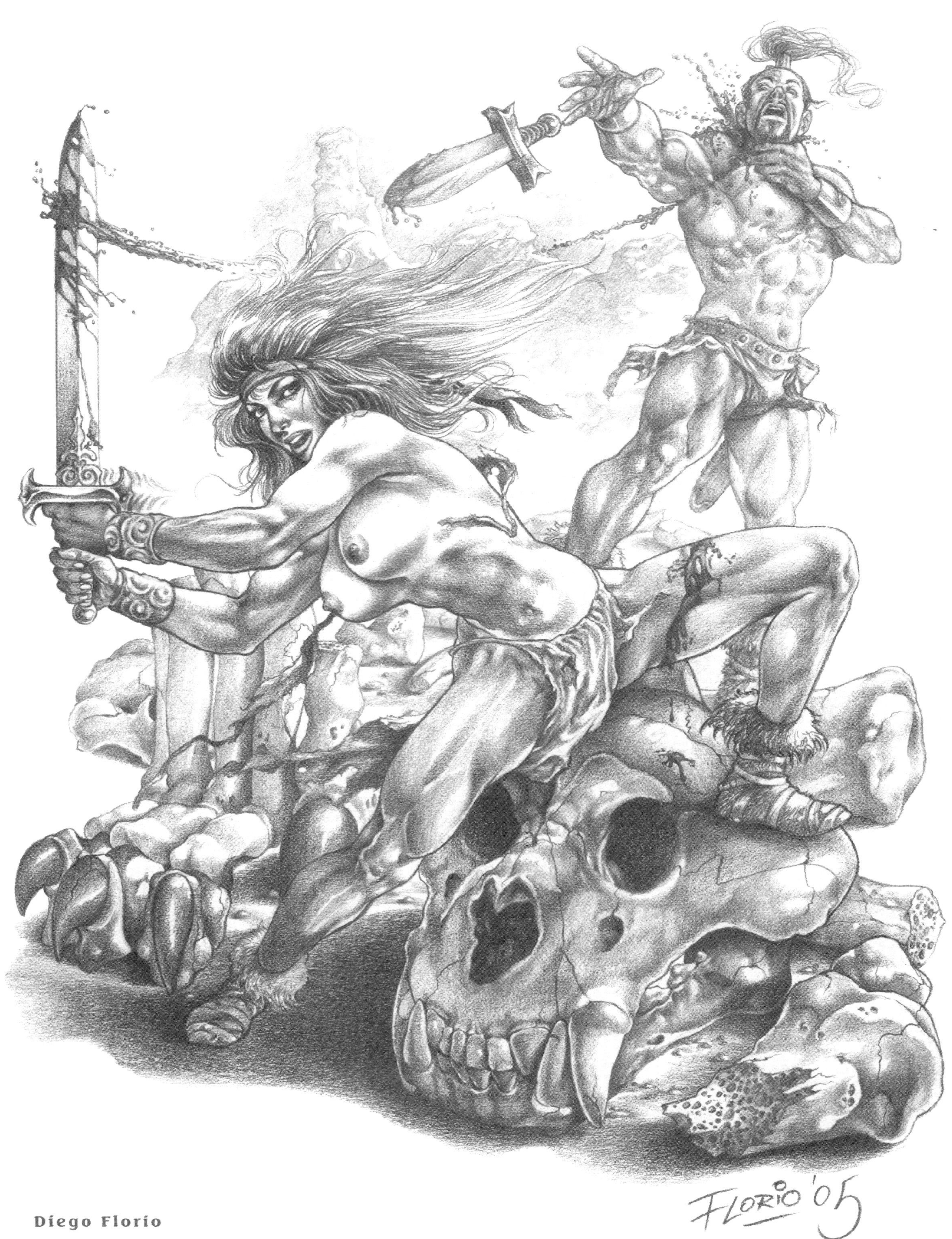

Diego Florio

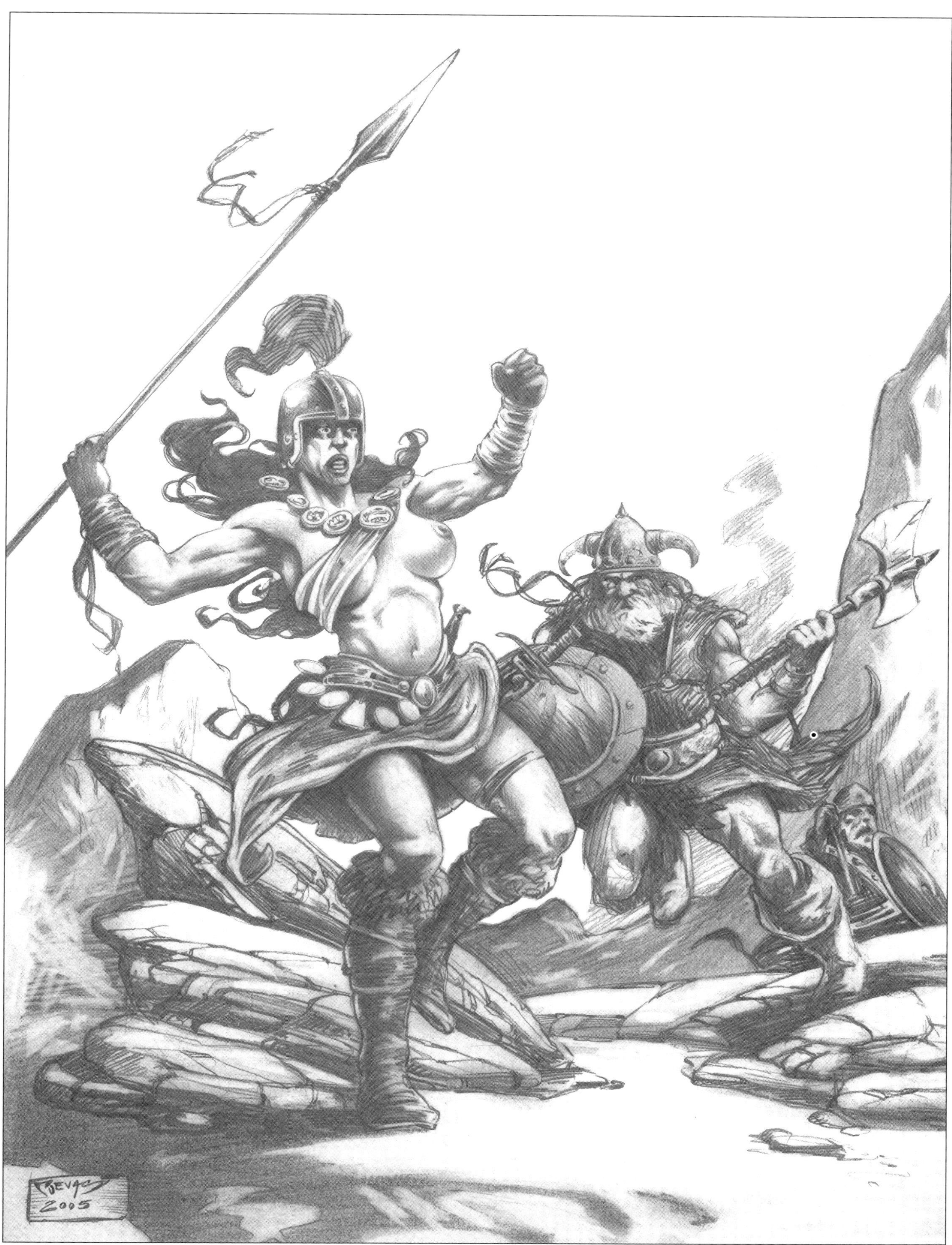

Pedro Cuevas

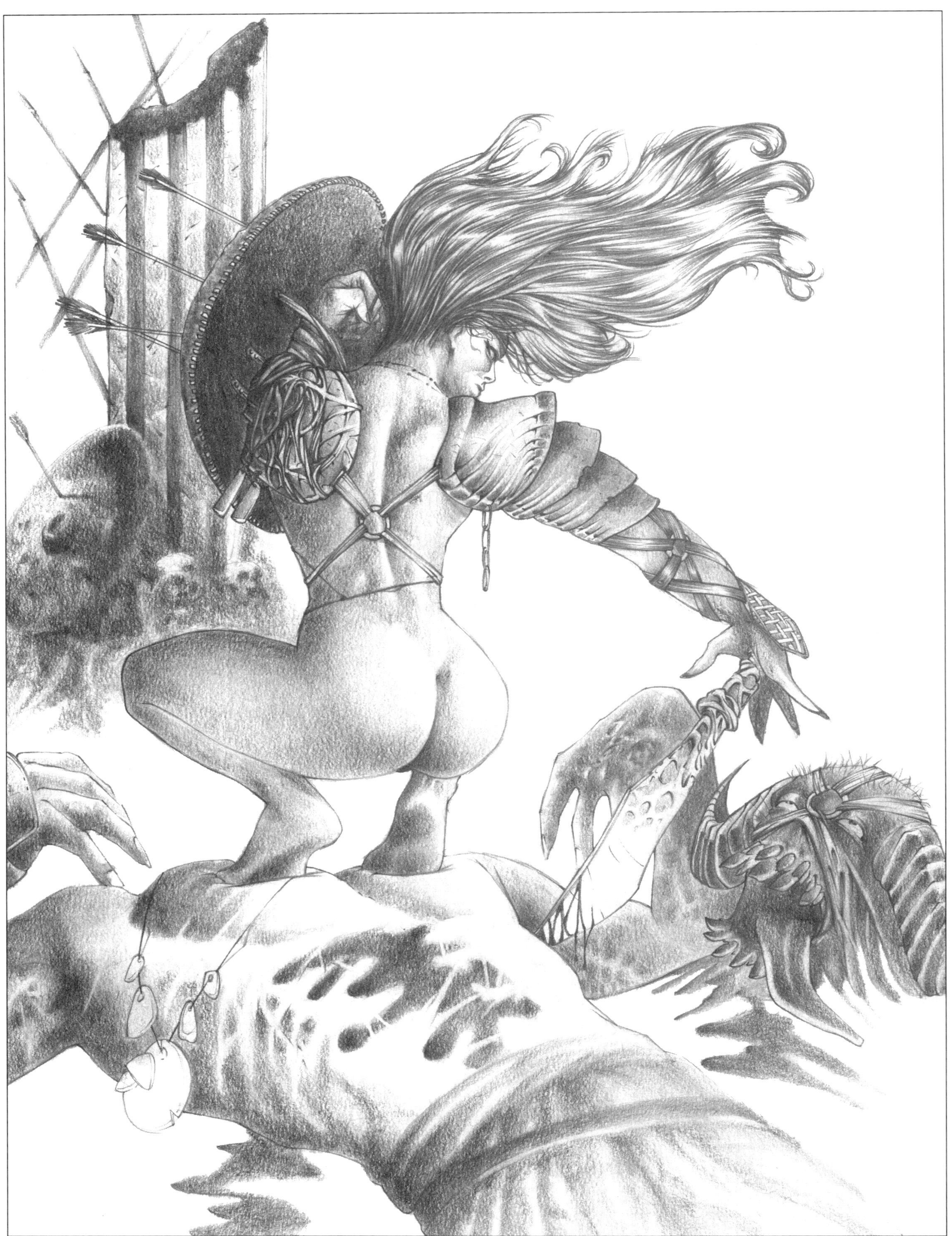

J.L. Czerniawski

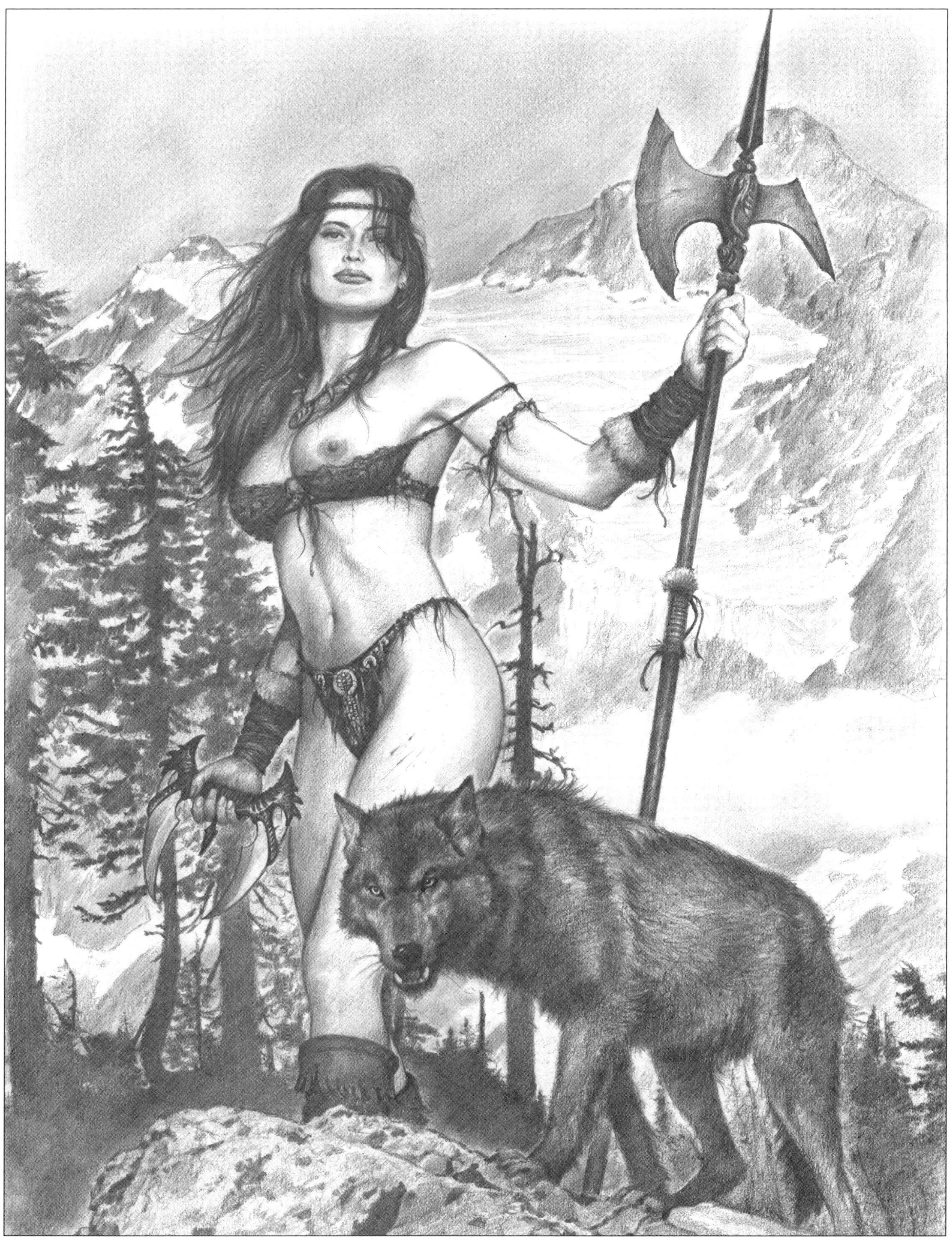

Pelaez

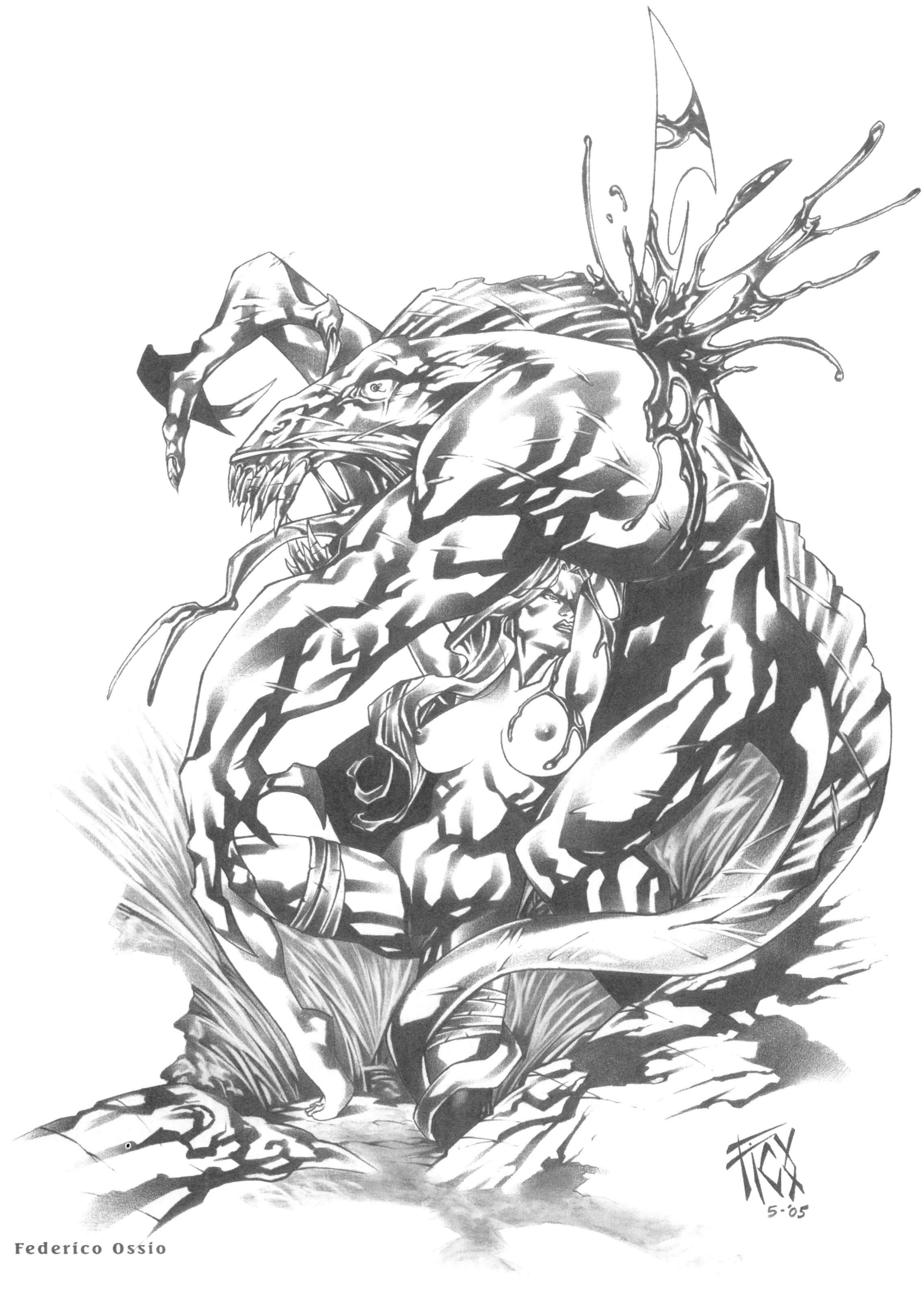

Federico Ossio

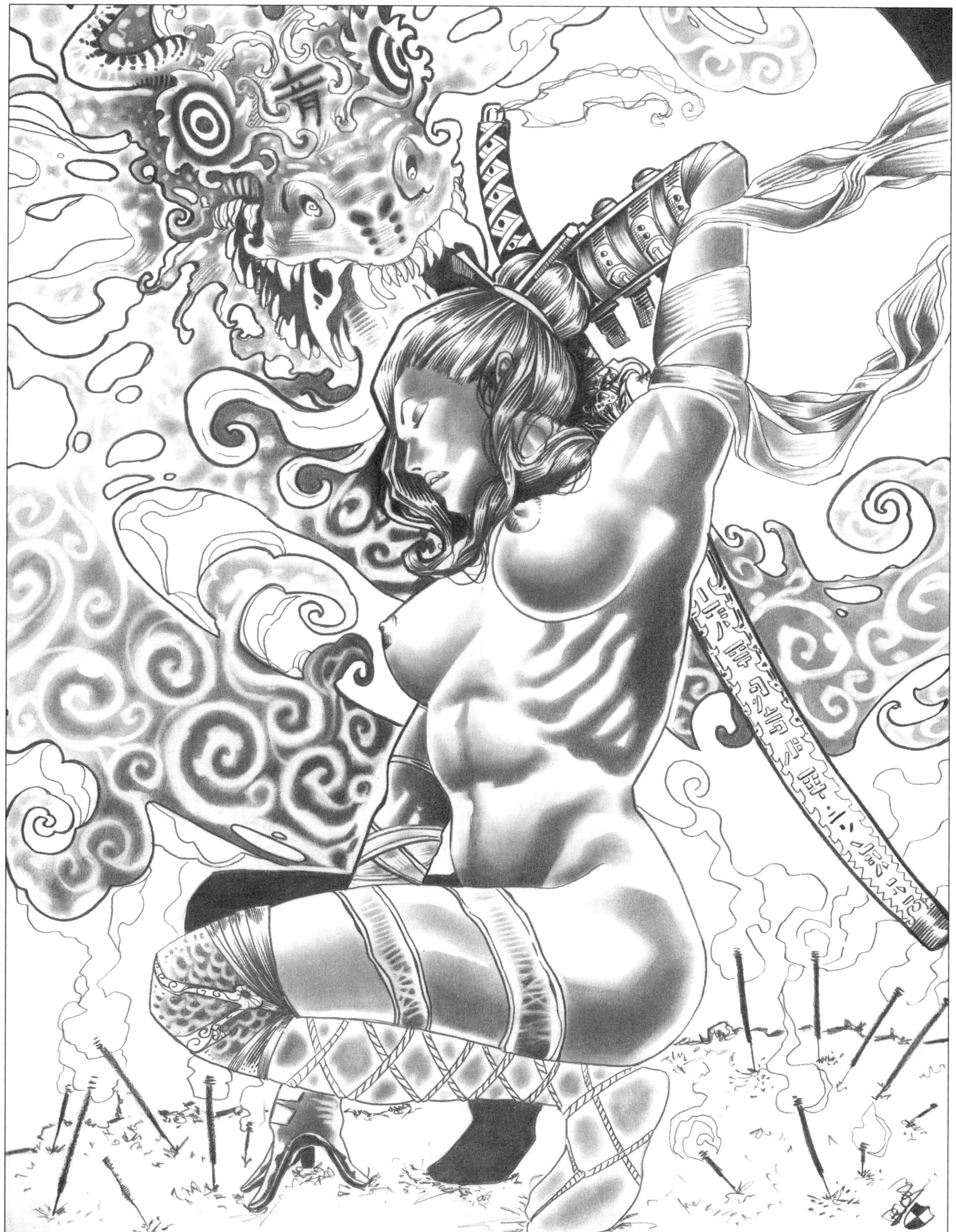

Luís Buci

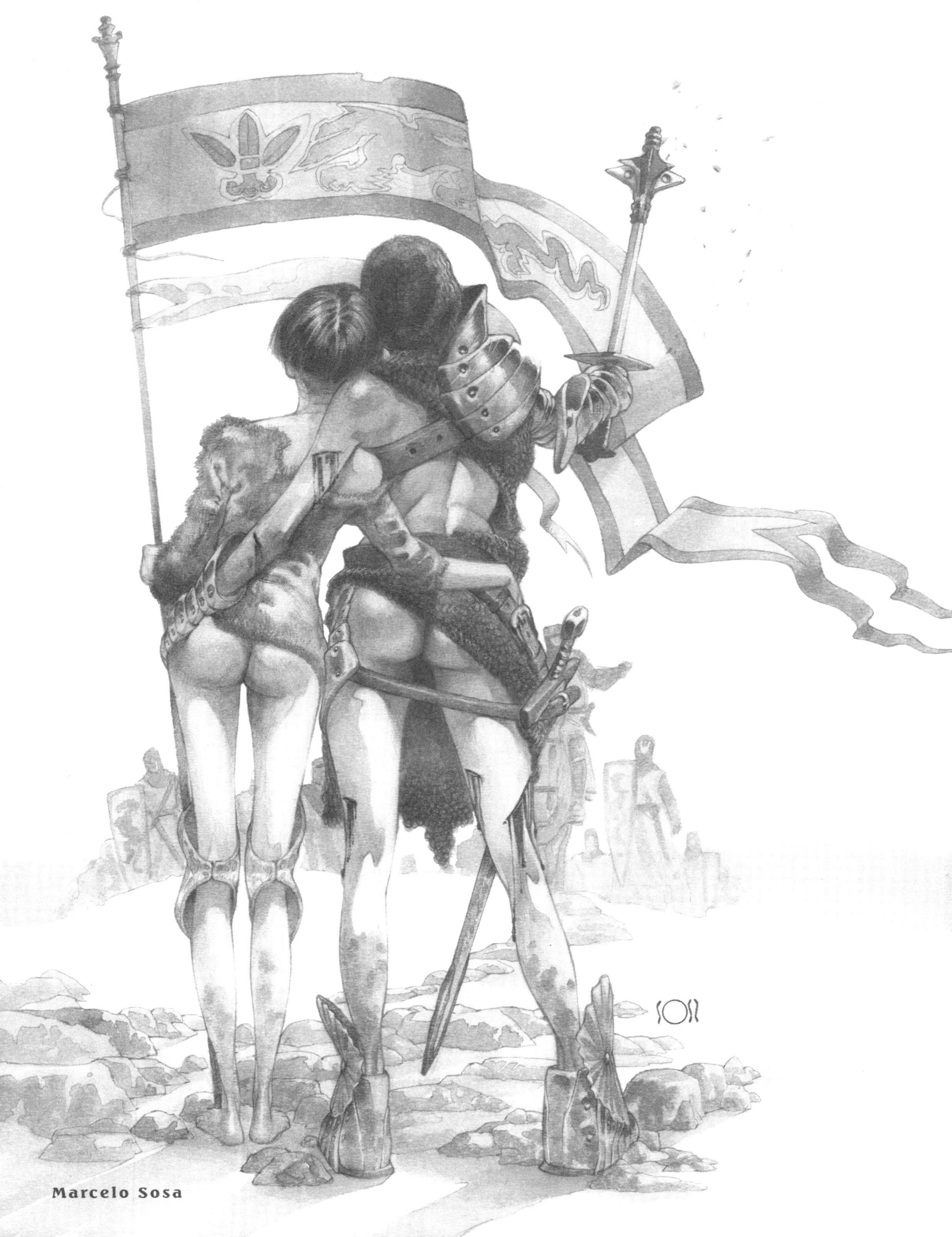

Marcelo Sosa